AN ADVENTURE WITH 2000+ ICONS, CURSORS, AND SOUNDS

ShadowCat Technologies

For book and bookstore information

http://www.prenha

'rentice Hall PTR
Saddle River, NJ
07458

Library of Congress Cataloging-in-Publication Data

```
Icon Safari : an adventure with 2000+ icons, cursors, and sounds /
   ShadowCat Technologies.
       p.  cm.
   Includes index.
   ISBN 0-13-459066-X (paper : alk. paper)
   1. Microsoft Windows (Computer file)  2. Icon safari.
   I. ShadowCat Technolgoies.
   QA76.76.W56I26  1996
   006.6'869--dc20                                          96-33973
                                                            CIP
```

Acquisitions editor: *Paul W. Becker*
Editorial assistant: *Maureen Diana*
Editorial/production supervision: *Patti Guerrieri*
Manufacturing buyer: *Alexis R. Heydt*
Cover design director: *Jerry Votta*
Cover designer: *Bruce Kenselaar*
Art director: *Gail Cocker-Bogusz*
Interior design: *Rosemarie Votta*

 ©1996 by Prentice Hall PTR
Prentice-Hall Inc.
A Simon & Schuster Company
Upper Saddle River, NJ 07458

The publisher offers discounts on this book when ordered in bulk quantities. For more information, contact:
Corporate Sales Department, Prentice Hall PTR, One Lake Street, Upper Saddle River, NJ 07458,
Phone: 800-382-3419, Fax: 201-236-7141, e-mail: corpsales@prenhall.com

Microsoft, Microsoft Windows, Windows 3.1, Windows 3.11, Windows NT, Windows 95 and the Microsoft
Plus! Pack are all trademarks of Microsoft Corporation. Earthwork Jim is a trademark of Shiny Entertainment.
All other products are trademarks of their respective companies.

Printed in the United States of America
10 9 8 7 6 5 4 3 2 1

ISBN   0-13-459066-X

Prentice-Hall International (UK) Limited, *London*
Prentice-Hall of Australia Pty. Limited, *Sydney*
Prentice-Hall Canada Inc., *Toronto*
Prentice-Hall Hispanoamericana, S.A., *Mexico*
Prentice-Hall of India Private Limited, *New Delhi*
Prentice-Hall of Japan, Inc., *Tokyo*
Simon & Schuster Asia Pte. Ltd., *Singapore*
Editora Prentice-Hall do Brasil, Ltda., *Rio de Janeiro*

Contents

Read Me First!!
Preface to the Preface of Icon Safari

(OK, it's silly to have a preface to a preface. But this is really important stuff—so read it!)

Icon Safari was originally designed for Windows 3.1; it has been upgraded and enhanced to run on Windows 95 (albeit with a few differences from the Win 3.1 version), and it also runs under Windows NT. However, there are some differences between the way it works under Windows 3.1 and the other versions of Windows. This table will help you understand the differences. There's also a quick question-and-answer guide immediately following this table to help you with some of the most commonly asked questions about Icon Safari.

Feature	Win 3.1, 3.11	Win95/Win NT	Win95 with Plus Pak
Icon Editor	Edits icons, cursors, bitmaps—works fine	Edits icons, cursors, bitmaps—works fine	Edits icons, cursors, bitmaps—works fine
Icon Animation	Works fine	Does not work (changes to the internal Windows system and prevents animation)	Does not work (changes to the internal Windows system and prevents animation)
Cursor Animation	Works fine	Works fine	Works fine if system cursor is standard. Bows out gracefully if system cursor is nonstandard.
Icon Viewer	Works fine	Works fine	Works fine
Sound Panel (Sound Player)	Works fine	Works fine; although Win95 provides access to some system sounds, the Sound Panel provides access to many more, including text buttons, which Win95 doesn't do at all.	Works fine; although Win95 provides access to some system sounds, the Sound Panel provides access to many more, including text buttons, which Win95 doesn't do at all.

FREQUENTLY ASKED QUESTIONS

▸ Why don't my cursors animate under Windows 95?

The most likely answer to this question is that you've got the Microsoft Plus Pak installed or have installed other color cursors into your system. Icon Safari has extremely sophisticated internal logic that recognizes that you've got something other than the standard system cursor installed and doesn't try to animate over that. (Doing so would make a great big ugly mess!) If you want to have Icon Safari animate the standard system cursor, but keep the other cool color cursors that you've got installed, do the following:

Setting the System Cursor to Standard, So That Icon Safari Can Animate It

1. Double-click (or otherwise open) your My Computer icon.

2. Select the Control Panel icon, and double-click to open it.

3. In the Control Panel window, double-click on the Mouse icon to open it. You should see the following dialog:

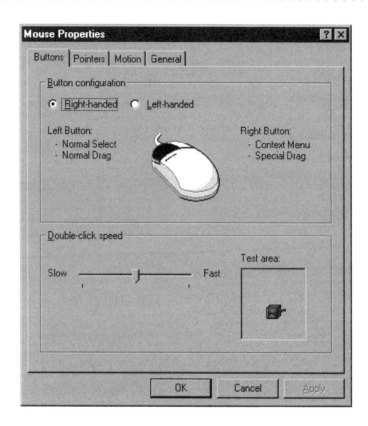

4. Select the Pointers tab on this dialog box, and you should see something like the following dialog:

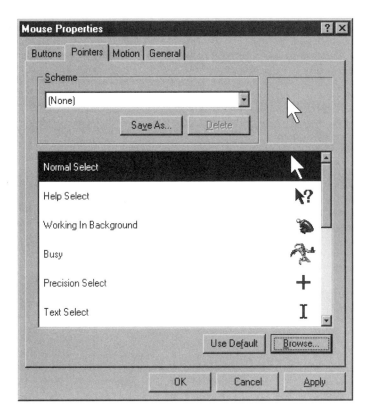

If the Normal Select cursor is not already selected, go ahead and select it. In this illustration, the Normal Select cursor has already been selected.

5. Click on the Use Default button just below the cursor list box. This will change the Normal Select cursor to the default system cursor. Then click on OK.

6. Your animations that are selected in Icon Safari's Cursor Control Panel will now show up for the standard system cursor.

7. If you want Icon Safari to animate the busy cursor, you'll need to set it to Use Default as well.

▶ The book mentions the pop-up program launcher, but I don't see it anywhere. Am I doing something wrong?

Nope. During the course of our development of this product for Win95, we discovered something—the pop-up program launcher caused Win95 to crash sporadically (that's a big word which means every so often, but mostly when you're not looking at it. <grin>). It works perfectly under Windows 3.1, and in theory, should have worked perfectly under Windows 95. It doesn't. It works—most of the time. Every so often, though, it causes an application running on 95 to crash. Because of this, we decided to ship Icon Safari with the pop-up program launcher turned **OFF**. If you're running Windows 3.1 and want to turn it on (or you're running Windows 95, and just feel lucky!), you can easily do so via the following procedure:

1. Launch the Icon Safari Navigator.

2. Click on the system menu button in the upper-left corner.

3. Select the Special Options menu entry. The following dialog comes up:

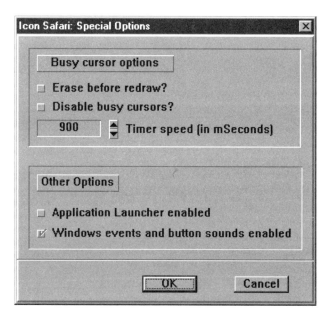

As you can see, under the Other Options section, the button labeled Application Launcher enabled has no check mark next to it—because the Application Launcher (the pop-up program launcher) is currently off.

4. Click on the check box so that a check mark appears in it.

5. Click on OK.

6. Icon Safari tells you that any changes you've made won't take effect until you shut down Icon Safari and rerun it. Go ahead and do that.

7. The pop-up application launcher should now be visible on the right side of the currently active window.

▶ I tried to load a .ANI file (or .CUR file), and I got a message that Icon Safari couldn't recognize the format. I tried to load the file anyway, and nothing happened.

This situation occurs because of a problem with file names with the .ANI extension—they aren't all the same *kind* of animation file. There are several different kinds:

.ANI—an animation file created with the Icon Safari editor and used by the Icon Safari Icon Animator and Cursor Animator control panels. This kind of file we read.
.ANI—an animated color cursor file, created with a third-party tool. This kind of .ANI file is shipped with the Microsoft Plus! pack, as well as third-party companies. Currently, the Icon Safari Editor and associated tools do not support this kind of animated file type.
.CUR—standard Windows cursor file. The Icon Safari Editor reads and writes this kind of file.
.CUR—an animated color cursor file. The Icon Safari Editor does *not* read this kind of file.

As you can see there are four different file types; despite the fact that they have the same file extension types, they are *not* the same kind of file. If the Icon Safari Editor (or other tool) posts a message indicating that it doesn't recognize the file in question, it means that the file is in a format that we don't understand.

[OK, that's the end of the really, really important stuff. The rest of this stuff is a short history of the product, people who helped make it a reality, and what kind of music I like to listen to.]

THE REAL PREFACE

This product that you have in your hands is the result of more than *ten years* of work. No kidding. I first started writing an Icon Editor way back in 1985 on the Atari ST. (OK, so I had my platforms a little confused. I'm over it now. <grin>) I ported it to Windows in 1990, basically rewriting it from scratch. From there it's grown into the tools you now hold.

Icon Safari started out as a magazine article for the now-defunct magazine *START*; I wrote the program (which was a lot simpler then) and I wrote the article to go with it.

As it turned out, enough people liked the article and program that I turned it into a little product; I added features, made improvements, and generally had fun with it. It was sold through the magazine and sold well for about a year. (Well is relative, of course. It never came close to paying for itself in terms of development time.)

With the ST marketplace dying a long, slow death, I decided to move onto greener pastures. In November 1990 I moved back to the MS-DOS and Windows 3.0 market. When I got there, I discovered that no one had available what I considered to be a good icon editor. (I figured I was entitled to an opinion, having written a pretty good icon editor myself.) Rather than use someone else's editor, I decided to port mine from GEM to Windows. This turned out to be a real learning experience, as well as decidedly nontrivial. In a short six months, I had a working version of Icon Editor. Then it took another two years to turn it into a commercial product. And then another two years...and *another* two years. These things take time, apparently...<grin>.

Because the Icon Editor and all the other pieces that are in Icon Safari are so goofy, a lot of people assume that there isn't much to them. Not true. The Icon Editor, and the associated tools that go along with it, comprise over *300,000* lines of C and C++ code. In between writing the code and writing the manual, I've managed to get some sleep. A little.

In the course of ten years, a few things have remained constant—my beautiful wife Shirley Ann, who grows more radiant with each passing day.

My sons Miles and Sloan, who weren't even a gleam in their dad's eye when I first set out to write an icon editor.

Other People Who Helped

The list of people who helped make this product a reality is almost too long to put down. Nevertheless, I'm going to try....

Steve Guty and Paul Becker (in the beginning and the end) at Prentice Hall were the editors on this product. They have shepherded this product through a long and difficult gestation, given lots of good advice, and made sure that a thousand little things were taken care of. They have my deepest thanks.

Maureen and Noreen, Paul's secretaries at Prentice Hall have been unfailingly cheerful when answering the phone, (even when they knew it was me). Thank you.

A big tip of the Hatlo Hat to my agent Matt Wagner at Waterside, who didn't give up, even after a full year of no results. Thanks, Matt!

A very big thank you to all the others at Waterside who supported me through this project, especially Maureen in accounting for the early Christmas present.

For leadership and vision (even when I really didn't want to hear it): Shirley A. Russell.

A huge number of people have made important design contributions to this product. It would not be as good as it is without their input:

Alan Cooper
Fran Finnegan
Kevin Goodman
Don Hackler
Nigel Hearne
Dave Korn
Bill Pryor
Shirley A. Russell
… and many others I'm sure I've forgotten.

Special thanks to Gary Yost and all the people who used to be at *START* magazine for the very original impetus for my writing an icon editor. If you'd told me then that ten years later I'd still be writing a version of it, I would have laughed in your face. Truth is stranger than fiction….

And last (but certainly not least) all the artists whose music I've listened to at extremely odd hours of the morning while working on this thing:

Boston
Queen
Tuck & Patti
Little Feat
ZZ Top
Joe Satriani
Steve Vai
The Who

And in the end, it's for the people who use this product that I've really written it—without you, this product really wouldn't exist.

Enjoy it—it's for *you*!

How to Contact Us

If you have requests for what you want to see in the next version of the software, like our product, don't like our product, or want to generally rant and rave at us, you can reach me electronically via CompuServe and the Internet at

Compuserve: 70444,43
Internet: alexleav@ix.netcom.com

or via the U.S. Post Office at

ShadowCat Technologies
2170 Waters Ferry Drive
Lawrenceville, GA 30243

Introduction

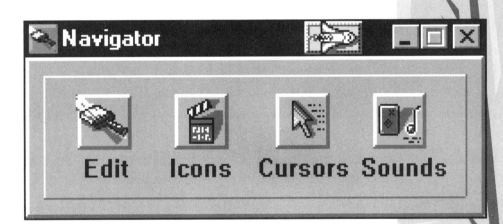

Icon Safari is a unique Windows software tool and toy that lets you customize your Windows desktop in lots of fun ways. You can use Icon Safari to do these things:

▶ View all the icons on your drives. This includes your hard drive, your CD-ROM drive and any floppies that you may have lying around.

▶ Animate your cursors.

▶ Attach sounds to lots of different Window actions, including moving, minimizing and maximizing, as well as hooking sounds up to more than 90 different buttons.

▶ Edit your own (or others') icons, cursors and bitmaps.

▶ Launch up to 15 of your favorite programs from the unique pop-up program launcher.

This book will show you how to do all of these things, as well as how to get the most out of this product.

The big piece of this product (depending upon how you view it) is the Icon Editor. It lets you create your own icons, cursors and small bitmaps. It also lets you edit other people's icons, cursors and bitmaps and save them out in new files. You can do cool things like change an icon into a bitmap, or a bitmap into a cursor, without much hassle at all. (In fact, assuming you've got your colors OK, changing a bitmap into a cursor takes exactly one mouse click.)

The Icon Safari Editor contains a whole host of neat editing tools, tools that are there because—well, because I *wanted* them there. I've been creating icons for a long time (you'll find a special subdirectory on your CD-ROM, under the Icons directory, labeled \alex that contains both icons and bitmaps that I've drawn using the Editor), and I'm in the unique position of not only wanting great editing tools for the creation of icons, but actually being able to do something about it. Many of the tools came about because I'd be editing an icon and say, "You know, I wish the Editor could do *this*..."—and then I'd sit down and make the Editor *do* this.

Many more tools, of course, came when *other* people would say, "You know, it'd be great if the Editor could do *that*." And after whining and moaning about how hard it would be to make the Editor do that, I'd usually sit down and do it.

In case you *don't* want to create your own icons, you'll find well over 2000 icons on the CD that comes with this book. You can use the Icon Viewer to look at all the icons you have available. If you want to edit one of the icons, just double-click on it, and it'll be brought into the Editor. I've tried to make sure that all the icons are unique, but I'm sure that a few duplicates have slipped through. (Just try staring at several thousand icons for any period of time, and you'll see what I mean.) In particular, I'm sure that some of the icons in the \icons\alex directory are duplicated elsewhere. Not to worry, though—with something like 4000+ icons on the disk, I'm sure you'll find some that you like.

You can also use the Icon Viewer to prune unwanted icons from your hard drive—just open a directory that has icons in it, and you can delete any you don't like.

The other pieces of silliness that are in the program are the Icon Animator (works only under Windows 3.1), the Cursor Animator and the Sound Player.

The Icon Animator lets you hook up icon animations that you can create with the Icon Editor—you'll also find plenty of them on the CD in the directory \iconani—to any icons on your desktop. I must emphasize—*this only works under Windows 3.1 and 3.11*. If you're using either Program Manager or the Norton Desktop for Windows, then the animation stuff will work fine. If you're running Windows 95, you're probably already grumbling. I know—I'm running 95, too, and it won't work for me either. (The long form of this answer is that Microsoft changed the way icons are handled from 3.1 to 95. As a result, all of the magical information that I was relying on in order to make animations happen went away. Sigh.)

So if you're running Windows 3.1, you can have neat icon animations on your desktop—if you're running Windows 95, you can't. (Sorry.)

Cursor animation, however, works perfectly well under both systems. You can assign monochrome cursor animations to your system cursor, your busy cursor and your idle cursor. If you've installed the Microsoft Plus Pak, you'll see that it contains color cursors—these are *different* things entirely from the monochrome animated cursors that Icon Safari supports. The good news is that they live together perfectly happily. If you've got color cursors installed via the desktop, the Cursor Animator won't mess with them. If you don't, then you can use the monochrome cursor animations that come on the CD (or you can create your own with the Editor).

Finally, the Sound Player also works beautifully on both Windows 3.x and Windows 95. It can attach sounds to different events, such as moving or resizing a window (something which Windows 3.x doesn't support, but Windows 95 does). Something that neither version of Windows supports is the ability to hook sounds up to text buttons (such as OK). The Sound Player lets you do that, too.

The pop-up program launcher lets you launch any of your favorite programs from any application on the desktop. The floating program launcher sits in the title bar of the active window and pops up whenever you click on it. From here, you can launch a favorite program (the default installation lets you launch a couple of programs, and you can easily add your own to the list), or add more programs to the launcher itself, as well as determine how the launcher button looks.

Some programs under Windows 95 don't like the pop-up program launcher—in particular, you tend to get program crashes, most notably in *other* programs. If this happens to you, you can turn off the pop-up program launcher from the Special Options menu of the Navigator. See Appendix A, What To Do If Something Goes Wrong, for more information on how to turn off the pop-up program launcher.

In addition to the programs that are installed from the CD, you'll also find a huge variety of sound files, bitmap images, cursor animations, icon animations and icons on the CD. I purposely do *not* install all of this stuff to your hard drive—because you might want the space for real things <grin>! Seriously, there is an enormous amount of stuff on the CD—browse through it and see what things you like—and then copy just those things to your hard drive. For example, you can preview all the sounds on the CD by using the Sound Control Panel and browsing your CD for the sound files (they're in \sounds). Once you find some sound files you like, you can copy them to the Icon Safari \snds directory (which was created when you installed the CD).

Now that you've gotten a brief overview of what's on the CD and what you can use it for, you can read the instructions on how to install the software from the CD, and then you can dive right into the meat of the book, which describes all of the tools in great detail.

INSTALLING ICON SAFARI

Installing Icon Safari under Windows 95 couldn't be easier! Simply insert the CD-ROM in your drive, and Windows 95 will take care of the rest by running the setup program for you. If the setup program *doesn't* start up, you can manually run the setup program by doing the following steps:

1. Double-click on the My Computer icon to open up the Navigator.

2. Double-click on your CD-ROM icon in the Navigator.

3. Double-click on the Setup icon in the window.

If the setup program doesn't run automatically, you can also troubleshoot what's wrong. (See Appendix A.)

Once you've gotten Icon Safari properly installed, you can run it by double-clicking on the Navigator.

1

The Navigator

The Navigator is the heart of Icon Safari. This is where you control all of the various fun things that Icon Safari can do. Take a look at Figure 1–1 to see a screen shot of the Navigator. As you can see, there are four main buttons which control your access to the various other aspects of Icon Safari. Here's how you access them.

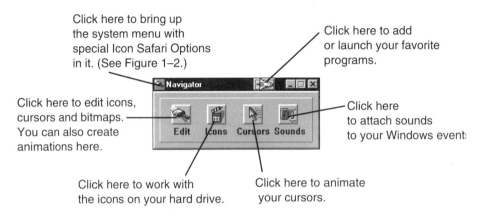

Figure 1–1 The Navigator Control Panel. You use this to control the other features of Icon Safari. In addition to the four main programs, Edit, Icons, Cursors and Sounds, you can also access special control functions by clicking on the system menu button (upper-left corner), or the pop-up program launcher (the shuttle button).

▶ To edit an icon, cursor or bitmap, click on the Edit button.

▶ To view icons on your hard drive, click on the Icons button.

▶ To animate your cursors, click on the Cursors button.

▶ To add sounds to your system, click on the Sounds button.

▶ To add programs to the pop-up program launcher, click on the shuttle.

The Navigator must be running for all of the cursor animations and sound playing capabilities to work. Normally, this should not be a problem, since this is the only program you should be running directly—all the other programs are accessed through the Navigator.

In addition to the main screen of the Navigator (see Figure 1–1), there are also several special control features that you can access. You

Click here to find out about
the Icon Safari Navigator.

Click here to enable or disable
special features of Icon Safari.

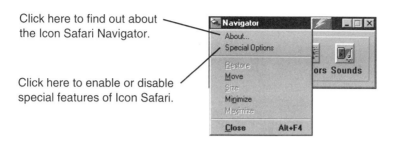

Figure 1–2 The System menu of the Icon Safari Navigator, showing the two
special entries that you can use to control Icon Safari.

can access these special features by clicking on the System Menu button
(in the upper-left corner of the main Navigator screen, see Figure 1–1)
and then clicking on the Special Options menu. See Figure 1–2 for a picture of what the System menu of the Navigator looks like. Figure 1–3
shows you the dialog box that you see when you select the Special
Options feature.

Check this button if your video card has problems
displaying the animated cursors used by Icon Safari.

Check this button if your video card has problems
(crashes or lock-ups) when trying to display
an animated busy cursor.

Check this button if you want the pop-up program
launcher enabled. (Using this feature can cause
intermittent crashes on some systems. If you
encounter such problems, uncheck this button.)

If you don't want system sounds to be enabled,
uncheck this button.

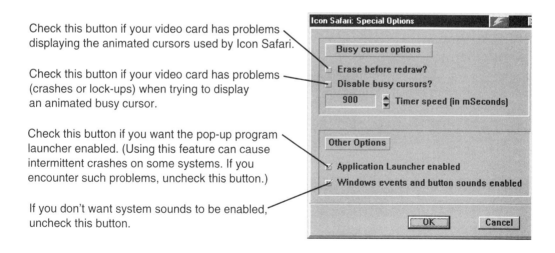

Figure 1–3 This is the control panel that comes up when you select the Special
Options menu in the system menu for the Navigator (see Figure 1–2). This
dialog allows you to control certain features of the Navigator which can affect
compatibility with your system.

Normally, you will not need to access these features. However, there are a few computers that have some incompatibility problems with some features of Icon Safari. In this case, you can turn off certain features of Icon Safari to resolve these compatibility problems. For further details on what problems might occur and what you can do to resolve them, see Appendix A.

Because of late-breaking compatibility problems with Windows 95, we ship the Navigator with the pop-up program launcher turned OFF. If you want to turn it back on, you'll have to go into the Special Options menu, described above.

Once the Navigator is up and running, you can use the special features of the different programs. In the following chapters, we'll explore the features of each of these areas in more detail.

2

The Icon
Viewer

The Icon Viewer program allows you to view all the icons that come with Icon Safari (as well as any other icons that you have on your system). The main window of the Icon Viewer is shown in Figure 2–1.

Click here to open icon files for viewing.

Click here to edit the currently selected icon.

Click here to delete the currently selected icon.

Click here to get info about the Icon Viewer.

The currently selected icon has this display box around it. You can select an icon by clicking on it. Double-clicking an icon will take you to the Icon Editor with the icon in it.

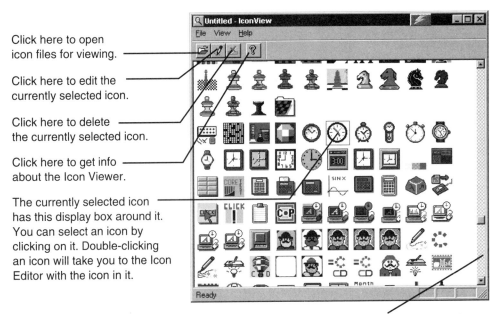

If there are more icons than can be viewed at one time, you can scroll through them with the scroll bar.

Figure 2–1 The Icon Viewer Control Panel. This tool lets you view icons on your hard drive, as well as edit and delete them.

When you first start up the Icon Viewer, the main window will be empty, because you haven't loaded any icons yet. To load icons, you'll need to do the following.

TO LOAD ICONS

1. Click on the Open File Folder icon on the menu bar, or select the Open… menu entry from the File menu.

2. A dialog similar to the one in Figure 2–2 will appear. This is the Windows 95 File Selection dialog. You can browse through your system using this dialog. Whenever the file dialog finds icon files, it will display them in a fashion similar to Figure 2–2.

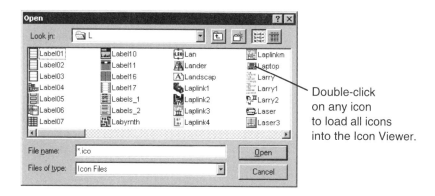

Figure 2–2 The Open File dialog that you get when you click on the Open File Folder, or on File…Open from the menu bar. Double-click here to select any icon, and all icons will be loaded into the Icon Viewer.

3. Double-click on any icon file in the file dialog. The Icon Viewer will automatically load all icon files in the directory and display them in the main window (see Figure 2–1).

Now that you've gotten your icons loaded, you can use the Icon Viewer to manage them. Here's what the Icon Manager can do for you:

▶ Let you view all the icons in a directory

▶ Get information about a selected icon

▶ Edit a selected icon

▶ Delete a selected icon

Most of the operations of the Icon Viewer rely on the notion of a "selected icon." This is simply the icon in which you're interested. Here's how you select an icon in the Icon Viewer.

TO SELECT AN ICON

1. Click on the icon you want to select.

2. A red box appears around the icon, indicating that it is selected.

Once you've gotten an icon selected, you can view its properties (what file name the icon is), delete it or edit it.

TO VIEW AN ICON'S PROPERTIES

1. Select an icon by clicking on it.

2. Select the Properties entry from the View menu *or* alternate-mouse click on the icon and select Properties from the pop-up menu.

3. The Icon Viewer will display a small dialog showing you what the file name of the icon file is.

TO EDIT AN ICON

1. Select an icon by clicking on it.

2. Select the Edit entry from the File menu (this entry will be grayed out if you do not have an icon selected) *or* double-click on the icon that you want to edit or *click* on the edit tool (the Pencil button; see Figure 2–1).

3. The Icon Safari Editor will be launched with the selected icon in the editing window. (See chapter 5 for more information about the Icon Safari Editor.)

4. You can now edit the icon.

TO DELETE AN ICON

1. Select an icon by clicking on it.

2. Select the Delete entry from the File menu (this entry will be grayed out if you do not have an icon selected) *or* click on the delete tool (the X button; see Figure 2–1).

3. A dialog similar to the one shown in Figure 2–3 will appear, asking you to confirm that you want to delete the selected icon.

4. Click on Yes to delete the icon, or click on No to abort the deletion.

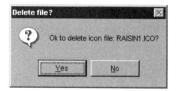

Figure 2–3 The dialog that appears when you delete an icon from the Icon Viewer.

3

The Cursor Panel

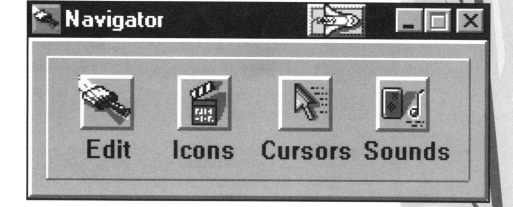

The Cursor panel allows you to apply animations to the windows cursors in a variety of ways. You can apply cursor animations to the following types of animations:

▸ Animation of the standard system cursor in any of eight directions.

▸ Animation of the standard system busy cursor, even when an application is processing.

▸ Animation of an idle cursor (one that has not been moved), similar to the way a screen saver works. (A cursor saver? <grin>)

See Figure 3–1 for a picture of the Cursor Control Panel. Once you've taken a look, we can talk about how you use the Cursor Control Panel.

When you start up the Cursor animation control panel, you'll see the default animation cursors selected for the eight degrees of motion. (By default, this is the walking hand that comes with Icon Safari.)

TO ANIMATE A MOVEMENT OF THE STANDARD SYSTEM CURSOR

1. Select an animation from the Cursor Animations list box (see Figure 3–1).

2. The animation will be displayed in the display box immediately to the right of the Cursor Animations list box.

3. If this is the animation you want, select one of the eight directions of the Mouse Cursor display panes:
   – up
   – up right
   – right
   – down right
   – down
   – down left
   – left
   – up left

4. The animation will be applied to that direction.

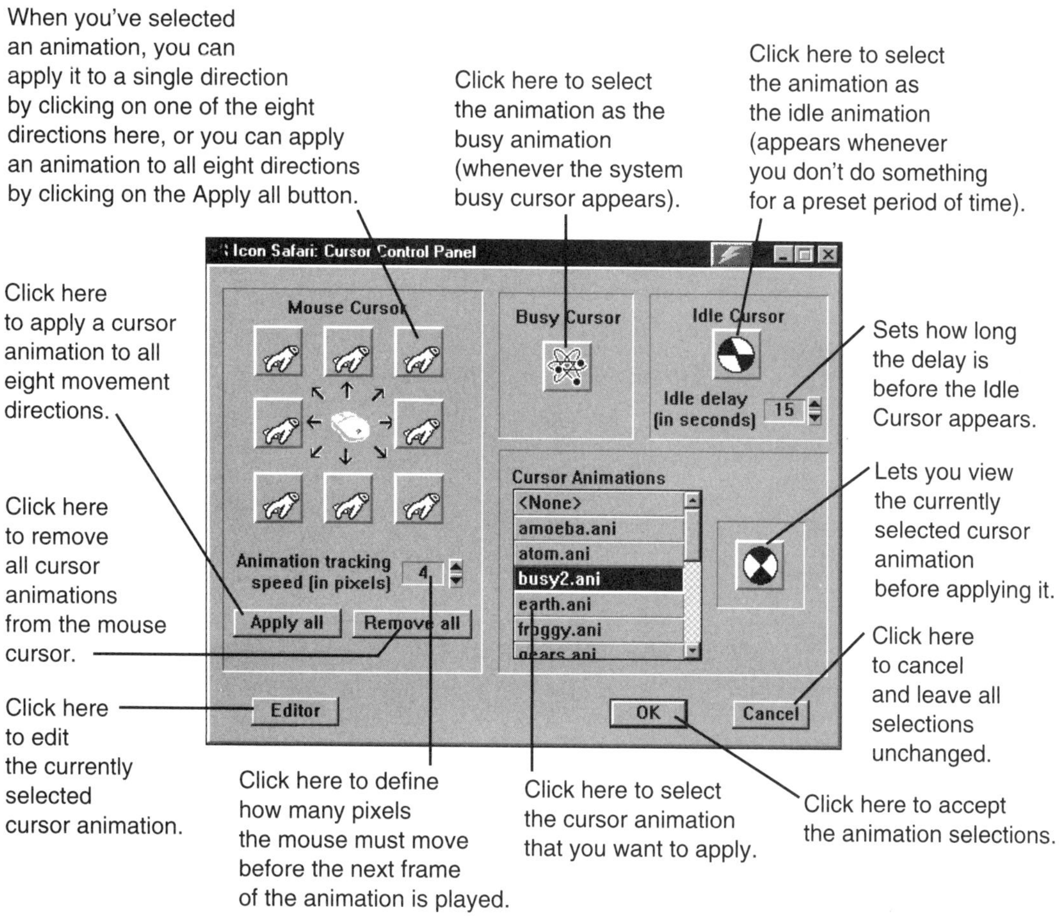

When you've selected
an animation, you can
apply it to a single direction
by clicking on one of the eight
directions here, or you can apply
an animation to all eight directions
by clicking on the Apply all button.

Click here to select
the animation as the
busy animation
(whenever the system
busy cursor appears).

Click here to select
the animation as
the idle animation
(appears whenever
you don't do something
for a preset period of time).

Click here
to apply a cursor
animation to all
eight movement
directions.

Sets how long
the delay is
before the Idle
Cursor appears.

Click here
to remove
all cursor
animations
from the mouse
cursor.

Lets you view
the currently
selected cursor
animation
before applying it.

Click here
to edit
the currently
selected
cursor animation.

Click here
to cancel
and leave all
selections
unchanged.

Click here to define
how many pixels
the mouse must move
before the next frame
of the animation is played.

Click here to select
the cursor animation
that you want to apply.

Click here to accept
the animation selections.

Icon Safari: Cursor Control Panel

Mouse Cursor

Busy Cursor

Idle Cursor

Idle delay
(in seconds) 15

Cursor Animations
<None>
amoeba.ani
atom.ani
busy2.ani
earth.ani
froggy.ani
gears.ani

Animation tracking
speed (in pixels) 4

Apply all   Remove all

Editor   OK   Cancel

Figure 3–1 The Cursor Control Panel. This control panel lets you set the options
that deal with animated cursors.

TO ANIMATE ALL THE MOVEMENTS OF THE STANDARD SYSTEM CURSOR WITH THE SAME ANIMATION

1. Select an animation from the Cursor Animations list box (see Figure 3–1).

2. The animation will be displayed in the display box immediately to the right of the Cursor Animations list box.

3. If this is the animation you want, click on the Apply all button in the Mouse Cursor display area. This will apply the same animation to all eight directions of motion of the system cursor.

TO ANIMATE THE SYSTEM BUSY CURSOR

1. Select an animation from the Cursor Animations list box (see Figure 3–1).

2. The animation will be displayed in the display box immediately to the right of the Cursor Animations list box.

3. If this is the animation you want, click on the Busy Cursor display pane. Now, when the system would normally display the hourglass, it will display this animation instead.

TO ANIMATE THE SYSTEM CURSOR WHEN IT IS IDLE

1. Select an animation from the Cursor Animations list box (see Figure 3–1).

2. The animation will be displayed in the display box immediately to the right of the Cursor Animations list box.

3. If this is the animation you want, click on the Idle Cursor display pane. Now, when the system cursor has not been moved for a period of time, it will begin playing this animation.

TO CONTROL HOW LONG IT IS BEFORE THE IDLE CURSOR ANIMATION APPEARS

1. To increase the amount of time it takes for the idle animation to appear, click in the up arrow next to the Idle Delay (in seconds) time display box. The idle delay time will increase.

2. To decrease the amount of time it takes for the idle animation to appear, click in the down arrow next to the Idle Delay (in seconds) time display box. The idle delay time will decrease.

3. Click in the time display box itself and enter a new number. This number is the time in seconds that the cursor must remain idle before the animation is played.

TO REMOVE AN ANIMATION FROM THE MOVEMENT OF THE STANDARD SYSTEM CURSOR

1. Select <None> from the list of cursor animations.

2. Select one of the eight directions of the Mouse Cursor display panes:
    – up
    – up right
    – right
    – down right
    – down
    – down left
    – left
    – up left

3. The animation will be removed from that direction.

TO REMOVE THE ANIMATIONS FROM ALL EIGHT DIRECTIONS OF MOVEMENT OF THE STANDARD SYSTEM CURSOR

1. Click on the Remove All button in the Mouse Cursor display area.

TO REMOVE THE ANIMATION FROM THE BUSY CURSOR

1. Select <None> from the list of cursor animations.

2. Click on the Busy Cursor display pane. The animation will be removed from the busy cursor. Now, when the system is busy, it will display the standard hourglass cursor.

TO REMOVE THE ANIMATION FROM THE IDLE CURSOR

1. Select <None> from the list of cursor animations.

2. Click on the Idle Cursor display pane. The animation will be removed from the idle cursor. Now, when the cursor has not been moved, the normal cursor will be displayed.

4

The Sound Control Panel

The Sound Control Panel allows you to control how and where sounds are used in your system. You can hook sounds up to four different types of events, so that whenever each event occurs, your sound will be played.

Here's an example. Suppose you want the computer to play the sound file ok.wav whenever you click on an OK button in the system. You can hook this wave file to the OK button and then the sound will be played whenever you click on an OK button, no matter what application the button is in.

There are four different kinds of events you can hook sounds up to (see Figure 4–1):

▶ Windows events

▶ Window actions

▶ Icon Safari Editor buttons

▶ Text buttons

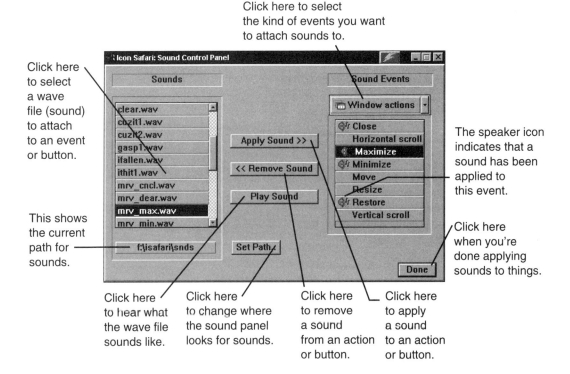

Figure 4–1 The Sound Control Panel. You use this to control how sounds are applied to different kinds of Windows system events.

Tables 4–1 and 4–2 describe each of these events and the circumstances under which they occur in more detail.

WINDOWS EVENTS

The standard Windows events are presented in Table 4–1.

Table 4–1

Windows start	Sound is played when you first start Windows.
Windows shutdown	Sound is played when you exit Windows.
Default beep	Sound is played when Windows plays the default sound.
Exclamation	Sound is played whenever a message box with an exclamation in it is displayed.
Asterisk	Sound is played whenever a message box with a red X in it is displayed.
Question	Sound is played whenever a message box with a question mark in it is displayed.
Critical stop	Sound is played whenever a critical stop is encountered.

WINDOW ACTIONS

The events that occur when you change a window's properties, or some-how manipulate the window are described in Table 4–2.

Table 4–2

Close	Sound is played whenever a window is closed using the close button or the system menu close command.
Horizontal scroll	Sound is played whenever a window is scrolled with a horizontal scroll bar.
Maximize	Sound is played whenever a window is maximized.
Minimize	Sound is played whenever a window is minimized.
Move	Sound is played whenever a window is moved.
Resize	Sound is played whenever a window is resized.
Restore	Sound is played whenever a window is restored.
Vertical scroll	Sound is played whenever a window is scrolled vertically with a vertical scroll bar.

ICON SAFARI EDITOR BUTTONS

These are events that occur whenever you click on one of the buttons in the Icon Safari Editor. Here is a list of all the buttons that can generate a sound if you have one hooked up. (The button functions are described in more detail in the chapter on the Icon Safari Editor.)

Arc	Grabber	Pencil Tool	Skew
Circle	Icon Library	Play	Snap Shot
Clear	Invert	Rectangle	Spray Paint
Eraser	Line Tool	Rotate	Stop
Fill Tool	Mirror	Select	Undo
Flip	Paint Brush	Shift	

WINDOW BUTTONS

These are events that occur whenever you click on a button in an application that has a particular label, such as OK or Cancel. Here is a list of all the buttons that can generate a sound if you have one hooked up.

Abort	Continue	Next	Save As
About	Copy	No	Search
Add	Create	OK	Send
Apply	Delete	Open	Set
Arrange	Done	Options	Settings
Assign	Edit	Pause	Setup
Back	Editor	Play	Show
Browse	End	Preview	Switch
Cancel	Exit	Previous	Test
Cascade	Files	Print	Tile
Change	Glossary	Remove	Undo
Change Icon	Go	Replace	View
Clear	Go To	Reset	Yes
Close	Help	Restore	
Color	History	Resume	
Connect	Insert	Retry	
Contents	Modify	Save	

Now that you've seen the types of events that you can hook sounds to, let's take a look at how you can actually hook up a sound to an event.

HOOKING A SOUND TO AN EVENT

1. Select the type of event that you want to hook a sound to from the Sound Events drop-down menu. (See Figure 4–2.) You can select from one of four kinds of events—System events, Window actions, Editor Tools, or Buttons.

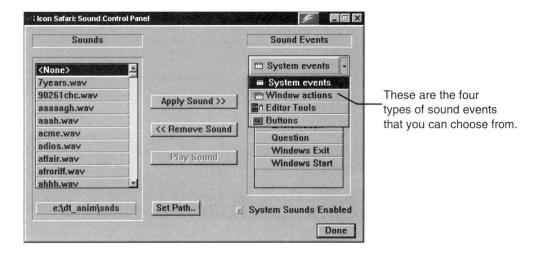

Figure 4–2 The Sound Events Display box. This control allows you to select what kinds of events you want to hook sounds to: System events, Window actions, Editor Tools, or Buttons within programs.

2. Select the actual event that you want to hook a sound to from the Sound Events list box (see Figure 4–1).

3. If the event already has a sound associated with it, it will have a small speaker icon displayed just to the left of the event. In this case, the sound that is associated with the event will be selected from the Sounds list box (on the left-hand side of the dialog). If there is no sound associated with the event (there is no speaker next to the event), then the entry <None> in the Sounds list box will be selected.

4. Select the new sound that you want to associate with the event from the Sounds list box.

5. Click on the Apply sound >> button.

6. The event will have a speaker icon placed next to it, indicating that the event now has a sound associated with it.

REMOVING A SOUND ASSOCIATED WITH AN EVENT

1. Select the type of event that you want to remove a sound from from the Sound Events drop-down menu. (See Figure 4–2.) You can select from one of four kinds of events—System events, Window actions, Editor Tools, or Buttons.

2. Select the actual event that you want to remove a sound from from the Sound Events list box (see Figure 4–1).

3. Click on the << Remove Sound button.

4. The event will have the speaker icon removed from it, indicating that there is no sound associated with this event.

PLAYING A SOUND

1. Select a sound from the Sounds list box on the left-hand side of the dialog.

2. Click on the Play Sound button.

3. The sound will be played.

TELLING THE SOUND PANEL WHERE TO LOOK FOR SOUNDS

1. Click on the Set Path... button.

2. A dialog allowing you to choose the path comes up (see Figure 4–3).

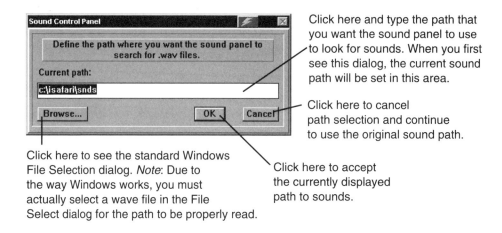

Click here and type the path that you want the sound panel to use to look for sounds. When you first see this dialog, the current sound path will be set in this area.

Click here to cancel path selection and continue to use the original sound path.

Click here to see the standard Windows File Selection dialog. *Note*: Due to the way Windows works, you must actually select a wave file in the File Select dialog for the path to be properly read.

Click here to accept the currently displayed path to sounds.

Figure 4–3 This dialog allows you to set the path that the Sound Control Panel will use to look for sound files. You get this dialog by clicking on the Set Path... button in the Sound Control Panel. (See Figure 4–1.)

3. To set the path directly, type the new path in the edit box.

4. To browse for wave files, click on the Browse... button. (See the next section for directions on how to browse for a new path.)

5. After the new path has been set, click on OK to accept the new path, or Cancel to reject it.

6. The wave files in the new directory will be displayed in the Sounds list box on the left-hand side of the dialog (see Figure 4–1).

BROWSING FOR A NEW PATH FOR SOUNDS

1. Click on the Browse… button in the Set Path… control dialog (see Figure 4–3).

2. The standard Windows File Selector dialog comes up (see Figure 4–4).

Note: You *must* click on a particular file here in order to properly select a file for the Set Path dialog. You can do this by either double-clicking on a file name or single-clicking the filename, and then clicking on OK.

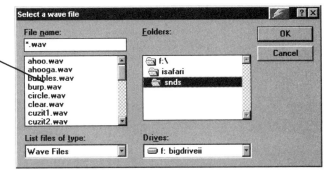

Figure 4–4 The File Select dialog box that comes up when you click on the Browse… button in the Sound Control Panel Set Path dialog. (See Figure 4–3.)

3. Choose the new path that you want.

4. Select a wave file from the new path. **IMPORTANT**!! You *must* select an individual wave file, or the dialog will not properly read the new path. (This is the way the dialog is designed, and is a function of Windows. We cannot affect this behavior.)

5. After selecting the wave file, click OK.

6. You will be returned to the Set Path… control dialog. (See Figure 4–3.) The new path will be displayed in the edit control. To accept this path, click OK in the Set Path… control dialog.

5

The Icon
Safari Editor

The Icon Safari Editor is an icon editor designed for programmers, software engineers, graphics artists and any others who find themselves needing a tool with which to create graphics images for Windows. (The Icon Safari Editor will create images that are compatible with Windows 3.x as well as Windows 95.) It provides a powerful editing engine for the creation of icons, cursors and bitmaps and allows you to save them in the proper format for inclusion in your or other people's programs.

The Icon Safari Editor also incorporates an Icon Library Manager, which allows you to view icons, cursors and bitmaps in various files such as .DLL and .DRV. It supports the Windows Clipboard and gives you what we feel is the most powerful set of image manipulation tools available anywhere.

To begin using the Icon Safari Editor, click on the Edit button in the Icon Safari Navigator (see Figure 1–1). This will bring up the Icon Safari Editor.

NOVICE VERSUS EXPERT MODE

The first time you run the Icon Safari Editor, it comes up in *Novice User* mode. In this mode, you are warned about many different types of actions which can alter or erase your work. As you become more familiar with the operation of the Editor, you can eliminate many of these warning messages by choosing the *Expert User* mode.

TYPES OF IMAGES YOU CAN CREATE

You can create five different types of images using the Icon Safari Editor:

▶ Bitmaps—Color images which can be used in a variety of ways: warning boxes, push buttons, and so forth. The only difference between a bitmap and an icon is that an icon has transparent and clear colors, and a bitmap does not. The maximum bitmap size available is 32x32.

▶ Icons—Color images displayed by the Windows desktop for different kinds of programs and file types. Icons can be 16x16, 16x32, 32x16 or 32x32.

▶ Cursors—Cursors are monochrome (black and white) images which represent the movement and actions of the mouse. The Cursor Control Panel can attach various cursors to different actions in the Windows system.

▶ Animated Bitmaps—Multiframe images which are played back, giving the illusion of motion.

▶ Animated Cursors—Multiframe images which are used to give the system cursor the appearance of motion.

Each of the five image types is created in the same way—you use the editing tools of the Icon Safari Editor to create your image and then save it in the appropriate format. Let's take a look at how you edit images in the Icon Safari Editor and what tools you have to help you create images.

INTRODUCTION TO THE EDITOR

Once the Icon Safari Editor begins execution, it displays the main editing window. This is the window where you will do most of your work, and it's broken into several areas. (See Figure 5–1.)

The Editing Grid

The largest area in the window is the Editing Grid. This is the area where you will actually construct your images. Each of the large cells in the Editing Grid corresponds to a single pixel in the final image, which is represented by the Image Preview, which is the small box to the top right of the edit window (see Figure 5–1). Every time you manipulate one or more of the large pixels in the Editing Grid, the corresponding change is reflected in the Image Preview window, allowing you to see how the resulting image will actually be displayed. The Image Preview window shows your image *at actual size*, so you can tell right away if the image you are building is what you want.

You can use the Show Mouse Position menu entry to display the cursor's current position in the Editing Grid. The position is shown in the status bar of the main window in (x,y) format. This means that the first number refers to the horizontal (left-right) position of the cursor, and the second number refers to the vertical (top-bottom) position.

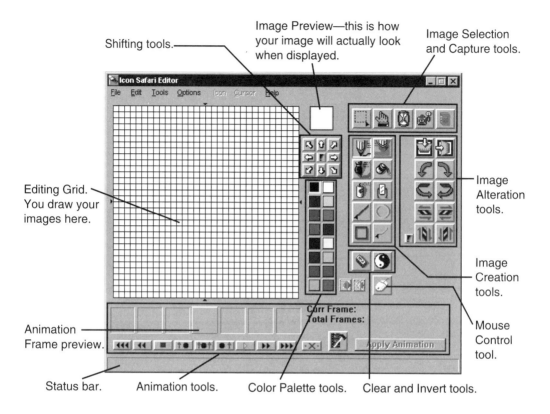

Figure 5-1 The Icon Safari Editor's Main Window. This is where you'll do the bulk of your work when you create different kinds of images.

FRAME PREVIEW

Not only does the Editing Grid have the Image Preview area for previewing single-frame images, it also has an animation workbench Frame Preview area. This area lets you view a seven-frame range of your animation. The breakdown of the Frame Preview is as follows:

▶ The three frames immediately preceding the current frame

▶ The current frame

▶ The three frames immediately following the current frame.

The raised frame in the middle is the current frame. Using the animation tools, you can add frames before or after the current image, or replace or remove the current frame. The frame number of the current frame is indicated to the right of the Frame Preview windows. The total number of frames in the animation is also indicated to the right of the preview windows. (See Figure 5–2.)

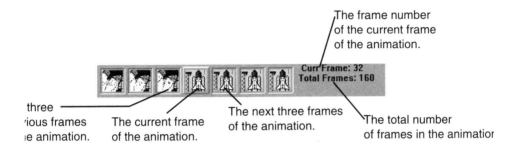

The frame number of the current frame of the animation.

Curr Frame: 32
Total Frames: 160

three
ious frames
le animation.

The current frame of the animation.

The next three frames of the animation.

The total number of frames in the animation

Figure 5–2 The Frame Preview window showing seven frames of the current animation, along with the current frame number and the total number of frames in the animation.

THE TOOLBOXES

The Icon Safari Editor has been designed so that tools that are logically related are physically grouped as well. For example, all the image creation tools are grouped together in the middle-right section of the main window (see Figure 5–1). This is because they all perform similar functions—they allow you to actually *create* pieces of the image that you're working on.

IMAGE CREATION TOOLS

There are nine image creation tools and one image creation modifier. (See Figure 5–3.)

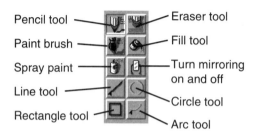

Pencil tool — Eraser tool
Paint brush — Fill tool
Spray paint — Turn mirroring on and off
Line tool — Circle tool
Rectangle tool — Arc tool

Figure 5–3 The Image Creation Tools. There are nine image creation tools, and one setting that modifies those tools. The tools are Pencil, Eraser, Paint Brush, Fill (paint can), Spray Paint, Line, Circle, Rectangle and Arc. The one modifier is the Mirroring tool.

The tools are these:

PENCIL TOOL   The Pencil tool is used to color single pixels or to draw free-form images. You can double-click on the tool to set its properties, or select the Set Pencil Tool… from the Tools menu.

ERASER TOOL   The Eraser tool erases rectangular portions of the image. You can set the size of the eraser by double-clicking on the tool, or by selecting Set Eraser… from the Tools menu.

PAINT BRUSH TOOL   The Paint Brush tool paints multiple pixel patterns at the same time using the selected color and brush pattern. You can set the brush pattern by double-clicking on the Paint Brush tool, or by choosing the Set Paint Brush entry from the Tools menu.

FILL (PAINT BUCKET) TOOL   The Paint Bucket tool fills in any closed shape or selected area with the selected color. You can set the behavior of the Paint Bucket tool by double-clicking the Paint Bucket tool, or by selecting the Set Paint Bucket entry from the Tools menu.

SPRAY PAINT TOOL   The Spray Can tool sprays multiple pixels at a certain flow rate of the currently selected color through the currently selected nozzle. You can set the nozzle pattern and flow rate by either double-clicking on the Spray Can tool, or by selecting the Set Spray Can entry from the Tools menu.

LINE TOOL   The Line tool creates straight lines. You can set the behavior of the line tool by double-clicking on the Line Tool button, or by choosing the Set Line Tool entry from the Tools menu.

CIRCLE TOOL   The Circle tool lets you create circles and ellipses in the currently selected color. Holding down the SHIFT key when drawing will constrain the program to drawing perfect circles. You can set the behavior of the circle tool by double-clicking on the Circle Tool button, or by choosing the Set Circle Tool entry from the Tools menu.

RECTANGLE TOOL   The Rectangle tool creates rectangles and squares in the currently selected color. Holding down the SHIFT key when drawing will constrain the program to drawing perfect squares. You can set the behavior of the Rectangle tool by double-clicking on the Rectangle Tool button, or by choosing the Set Rectangle Tool entry from the Tools menu.

ARC TOOL   The Arc tool creates arcs. Holding down the SHIFT key when drawing will constrain the program to drawing perfectly circular arcs (quarter of a circle). You can set the behavior of the Arc tool by double-clicking on the Arc Tool button, or by choosing the Set Arc Tool entry from the Tools menu.

MIRROR TOOL   The Mirror tool turns mirroring on or off. You can use the Mirror tool in conjunction with any of the other drawing tools, with the exception of the flood fill (Paint Bucket) tool. Mirroring has no effect on the Paint Bucket tool. When mirroring is turned on, whatever you draw is reflected (mirrored) about seven different possible axes of rotation. To set the behavior of the mirroring, double-click on the Mirror tool, or select Set Mirror tool from the Tools menu.

IMAGE ALTERATION TOOLS

The image alteration tools allow you to manipulate the image currently in the Editing Grid. These tools do not create any pixels but merely alter the pixels that are already there. All of these tools work on either the full image, or, if a portion of the image is selected (see Image Selection later in this chapter), then only on that portion of the image which is selected (see Figure 5–4).

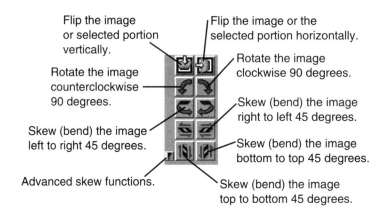

Flip the image or selected portion vertically.

Rotate the image counterclockwise 90 degrees.

Skew (bend) the image left to right 45 degrees.

Advanced skew functions.

Flip the image or the selected portion horizontally.

Rotate the image clockwise 90 degrees.

Skew (bend) the image right to left 45 degrees.

Skew (bend) the image bottom to top 45 degrees.

Skew (bend) the image top to bottom 45 degrees.

Figure 5–4 Image Alteration Tools. These tools let you flip, rotate and bend the image in a variety of ways.

FLIP TOOLS The Flip tools flip the image either horizontally (left to right) or vertically (top to bottom). They work on either the full image or the currently selected portion of the image (if there is one).

ROTATE TOOLS The Rotate tools rotate the image either clockwise or counterclockwise in increments of either 90 degrees or 180 degrees. They work on either the full image or the currently selected portion of the image (if there is one).

SKEW (BEND) TOOLS The Skew tools allow you to skew, or bend, the image in a variety of ways. You can bend the image left to right or right to left, in 45-degree increments, and you can bend the image top to bottom or bottom to top in 45-degree increments. Additionally, you can bend the image in other increments by clicking on the Exclamation Mark button next to the Skew tools, or by selecting Skew Tool from the Tools menu.

SHIFTING TOOLS The Shift tools allow you to move the image around in case it isn't quite where you want it. The image (or a selected portion) can be shifted in any of eight possible directions via the arrows. For additional shifting capabilities, click on the Exclamation Mark button in the center of the shift tools. This allows you to control how the image is shifted, how many pixels each shift takes up, and several other options. (See Figure 5–5 for the fast shifting tools and Figure 5–6 for the more complete controls.)

Figure 5–5 The shifting tools, which allow you to shift the image, or a selected portion, around the screen.

In the dialog, you can use the shift keys to move the image around, just as you can in the main image. However, the more important controls are those which define how many pixels each shift covers, and whether or not to wrap the image.

NUMBER OF PIXELS This defines how many pixels the image will be moved each time a shift button is clicked. It can be any number from 1 to 32. The default is 1.

WRAP IMAGE? If this button is checked, then the image (or selected portion of it) is treated as a torus—when a pixel being shifted hits an edge and falls off, it is wrapped around to the other side. If the button is not checked, then any pixel which hits an edge and falls off is lost.

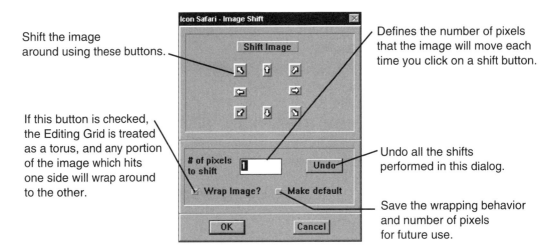

Shift the image around using these buttons.

Defines the number of pixels that the image will move each time you click on a shift button.

If this button is checked, the Editing Grid is treated as a torus, and any portion of the image which hits one side will wrap around to the other.

Undo all the shifts performed in this dialog.

Save the wrapping behavior and number of pixels for future use.

Figure 5–6 The control panel that you get when you click on the Exclamation Mark button in the center of the shift tools. This dialog lets you control the amount of shifting that occurs, as well as buffer the shifts that you do, in case you want to test something out.

COLOR PALETTE TOOLS

The Color Palette (see Figure 5–7) allows you to select the color used by the Image Creation tools, so it's located near them. Click on the color you want used for subsequent graphics operations; the color you clicked on will "shrink" into the center of its square, indicating that it has been chosen. (Note: When editing icons and cursors, you also have two additional colors—clear and inverse—that you can use. These colors are available directly to the right of the main color palette. When you are editing bitmaps, these buttons are disabled.)

The color *transparent* (see Figure 5–7) allows you to use any of the drawing tools to create a transparent area in your image. When the transparent color is used, that area of the icon or cursor becomes see through and allows the background or window to show through. Transparent pixels are displayed on the Editing Grid as white squares with left diagonal lines running through them (see Figure 5–8).

The color *inverse* (see Figure 5–7) allows you to use any of the drawing tools to create an area of inverted color in your image. When the inverse color is used, that area of the icon or cursor becomes "inverted" and allows the background or window to show through, but in the

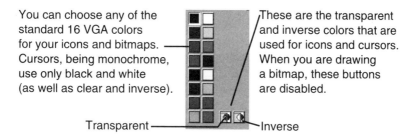

You can choose any of the standard 16 VGA colors for your icons and bitmaps. Cursors, being monochrome, use only black and white (as well as clear and inverse).

These are the transparent and inverse colors that are used for icons and cursors. When you are drawing a bitmap, these buttons are disabled.

Transparent ——————————— Inverse

Figure 5-7 The Color Palette Tool. At all times, this tool shows what the currently selected drawing color is. All drawing operations that occur use this selected color.

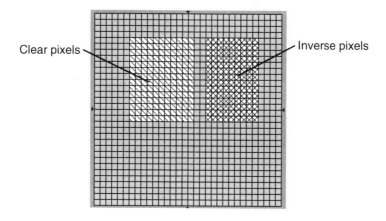

Clear pixels

Inverse pixels

Figure 5-8 An image showing two swatches, one transparent, one inverse, in an image.

opposite color of what would show through if the area were transparent. Inverse pixels are displayed on the Editing Grid as white squares with diagonally hatched lines running through them (see Figure 5–8).

IMAGE SELECTION AND CAPTURE TOOLS

The image selection and capture tools are used to select part of an image, capture an image off the screen, undo an image and more. (See Figure 5–9.)

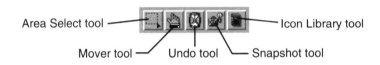

Area Select tool —————— Icon Library tool

Mover tool — Undo tool — Snapshot tool

Figure 5–9 Image Selection and Capture Tools. You use these tools to select parts of an image, or undo some of your work.

AREA SELECT TOOL The Area Select tool allows you to select a portion of the image for manipulation with any control or drawing tools, or the Full Clear tool. You can use this tool in conjunction with the shift key to constrain the selection area to a rectangle.

Double-click on the Area Select tool to specify whether you want the Area Select tool to automatically shift to the Mover tool once an area has been selected.

MOVER TOOL The Mover tool allows you to grab and move a selected portion of your image. Double-clicking on the tool, or choosing Set Mover Tool from the Tools menu will display a dialog containing additional options for moving your image.

UNDO TOOL The Undo tool undoes your previous action. You can click this tool up to five times to undo the last five operations.

SNAPSHOT TOOL   The Snapshot tool takes a 32x32 pixel snapshot of any image on the screen and displays it in the Editing Grid. When you use this tool, the Icon Safari Editor will minimize itself, revealing the window desktop and any other images that are there, allowing you to capture almost anything.

ICON LIBRARY TOOL   The Icon Library tool brings up the icon library, a dialog that allows you to view the icons, cursors and bitmaps contained in various program files and other places.

OTHER TOOLS

FULL CLEAR TOOL   The Full Clear tool clears the entire image on the Editing Grid, or, if an area is selected, clears only the selected portion of the image (see Figure 5–10).

Full Clear tool. Erases all or part of the image.

Invert tool. Inverts all or part of the image.

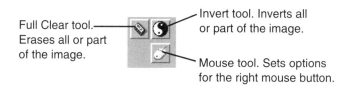

Mouse tool. Sets options for the right mouse button.

Figure 5–10 Icon Safari's Other Tools. The blackboard eraser will erase all or part of the image, the Yin-Yang button will invert the image, and the mouse button allows you to set mouse properties.

If you are in Novice user mode, you will be cautioned about clearing the workspace; if you are in Expert user mode, the work space is cleared without warning. (Don't worry, you can click on the Undo button to revert back to the image the way it was before you cleared it.)

INVERT TOOL   The Invert tool inverts the colors in the current image or selected portion. Inverse colors are located next to each other in the Color Palette. For example, black is the inverse of white and vice versa, dark red is the inverse of bright blue and vice versa, and so forth.

If you are in Novice mode, you will be cautioned about performing this operation. If you are in Expert mode, the action occurs immediately.

MOUSE CONTROL The Mouse Control tool brings up a dialog which allows you to set the behavior of the right mouse (more correctly, the alternate mouse) button. (See Figure 5–11.)

Click on one of these buttons to define how the right mouse button behaves.

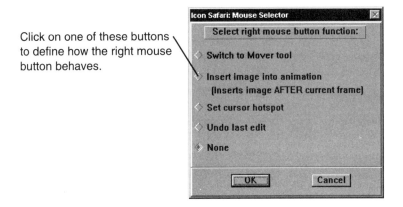

Figure 5–11 The dialog you get when you select the Mouse Control tool. You can control the function of the right mouse button with this dialog.

You have a choice of using the right mouse button for the following:

▶ Switching to Mover tool

▶ Setting cursor hotspot

▶ Adding the current image to the current animation

▶ Undoing the last edit

▶ No function

ANIMATION TOOLS

The animation tools are what you use when you are creating and editing animations. (See Figure 5–12.) These tools are used to play, create, add to and delete individual frames from an animated icon or cursor. The animation controls strongly resemble VCR controls, allowing you to move forward and backward through your animation.

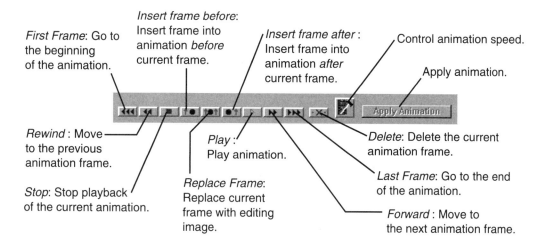

First Frame: Go to the beginning of the animation.

Insert frame before: Insert frame into animation *before* current frame.

Insert frame after : Insert frame into animation *after* current frame.

Control animation speed.

Apply animation.

Rewind : Move to the previous animation frame.

Play : Play animation.

Delete: Delete the current animation frame.

Stop: Stop playback of the current animation.

Replace Frame: Replace current frame with editing image.

Last Frame: Go to the end of the animation.

Forward : Move to the next animation frame.

Figure 5–12 The Animation Tool Workbench. You can control all the aspects of your animation work from here.

FIRST FRAME This button returns the animation to the first frame.

REWIND This button rewinds (steps backwards) through the animation, one frame at a time.

STOP Stops playback of the current animation. If the animation is not playing, this control has no effect.

INSERT FRAME BEFORE This button inserts the image from the Editing Grid into the animation directly *before* the current frame.

REPLACE FRAME This button replaces the current frame with the image from the Editing Grid.

INSERT FRAME AFTER This button inserts the image from the Editing Grid into the animation directly *after* the current frame.

PLAY This button starts playback of the current animation. The animation is displayed in the current frame window.

FORWARD This button advances (moves forward) through the animation, one frame at a time.

LAST FRAME This button moves the animation to the last frame.

DELETE This button deletes the current frame.

6

Using the Image Creation Tools

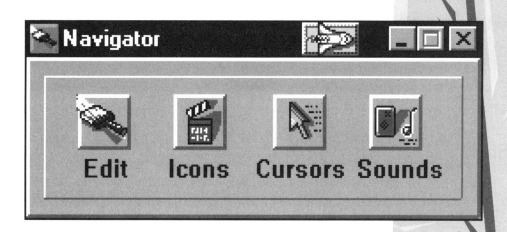

This chapter discusses in detail each of the drawing tools and how you can get the most out of them in creating your images.

THE PENCIL TOOL

The Pencil tool is the basic drawing tool of Icon Safari Editor. It draws single pixels in the current color as long as the left mouse button is held down. This means that you can not only point and click at single pixels with the pencil, but that you can also use it to draw freehand objects as well.

 Tip of the pencil defines where new pixels will be drawn.

The Pencil tool also has an eraser built into it. If you want to *erase* pixels (that is, paint in white), click on a pixel of the currently selected color and start drawing. In erase mode, Icon Safari Editor will replace any colored pixels that you move the pencil over with white ones. We think you'll find that combining the eraser function with the Pencil tool is quicker and more convenient than having a separate eraser tool.

Some people do not like having an integrated eraser in the Pencil tool. In this case, you can turn off the eraser by either double-clicking on the Pencil tool itself or by clicking on the Set Pencil Tool... entry of the Tools menu. This brings up the dialog shown in Figure 6–1.

 **Artist's Tip:** The Pencil tool, unlike many other paint programs, does *not* skip pixels. To get a "skipped pixel" effect, use the spray can tool, the single hole nozzle, and a low nozzle flow rate.

Click here to turn off
the eraser feature
of the Pencil tool.

Figure 6–1 The Pencil Tool Options Dialog Box. You can choose to turn off the eraser feature of the pencil by selecting the check box.

TO DRAW ON THE EDITING SURFACE

1. Select the Pencil tool.

2. Place the pencil cursor on the editing area at the spot where you want to draw.

3. Click the main mouse button (usually the left mouse button) and hold it down. The color that you are clicking down on should not be the same color as the currently selected color; otherwise you will be erasing the image rather than drawing on it.

4. Move the mouse in the shape that you want to draw.

TO ERASE PIXELS FROM THE EDITING SURFACE

1. Select the Pencil tool.

2. Place the pencil cursor on the editing area at the spot where you want to erase. This pixel must be the same color as the currently selected color.

3. Click the main mouse button (usually the left mouse button) and hold it down.

4. Move the mouse in the shape that you want to erase. All pixels that the cursor moves over (not just pixels of the current color) will be erased.

THE ERASER TOOL

The Eraser tool lets you remove parts of your image. The eraser's shape is always rectangular, but its size can be changed by double-clicking on the Eraser tool, or by selecting Set Eraser… from the Tools menu. Doing this brings up the dialog shown in Figure 6–2.

Set the size of the eraser by clicking on a size button here.

Select the behavior of the eraser by clicking on one of these three choices.

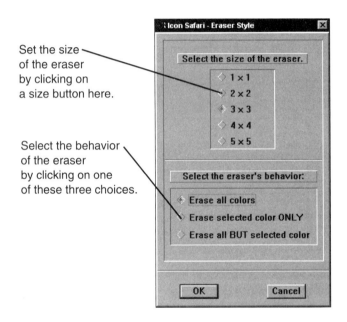

Figure 6–2 The Eraser Options Dialog. You can control the size of the eraser, from a rectangle 1 pixel big to a rectangle 5x5 pixels big (this will erase 25 pixels at a time). You can also choose how colors are erased: all colors, the selected color, or everything but the selected color.

You can control two things in the Eraser options dialog—the size of the eraser and how the eraser behaves.

The size of the eraser is quite straightforward—the eraser itself is a rectangle, and you control how big it is on a side. If the eraser is 1 pixel big, then it will erase only 1 pixel at a time. If the eraser is 2 pixels big (on a side), then it will erase 4 pixels. If it is 3 pixels on a side, it will erase 9 pixels, and so on, up to 5 pixels on a side, at which point it will erase 25 pixels each time you move it.

The other feature of the eraser that you control is what it erases. Normally, the eraser will always erase *all* the pixels that you move it over. However, in some cases, you don't want it to do this. Under these circumstances, you can change how it behaves by using one of two settings:

▶ Erase the selected color only

▶ Erase everything *but* the selected color.

In the first case, the eraser will erase only pixels which are the same color as your currently selected color. Thus, if you had (for example) dark blue selected as your drawing color, the eraser would erase only pixels which were dark blue. This can be handy for removing parts of an image which are not the right color, but whose shape you like.

In the second case, the eraser will erase all pixels which do *not* match the currently selected color. Thus, if you had (for example) green as your selected color, the eraser would erase all pixels *except* the green ones.

TO ERASE PARTS OF AN IMAGE

1. Select the Eraser tool.

2. Move the cursor to the point on the Editing Grid that you want to start erasing.

3. Click the main mouse button (usually the left mouse button) and hold it down.

4. Move the mouse in the shape that you want to erase. All pixels that the cursor moves over (not just pixels of the current color) will be erased.

THE PAINT BRUSH TOOL

The paint brush, like the pencil, lets you paint colored pixels onto the Editing Grid. But while the pencil only lets you paint a single pixel at a time, the paint brush lets you paint multiple pixels, in one of 10 selectable *brush patterns*. You can set which paint brush pattern will be used by double-clicking on the Paint Brush, or by choosing the Set Paint Brush menu entry from the Tools menu.

To select one of the brushes, first single-click on the Paint Brush button and then on OK. You can also select a brush by double-clicking on the Paint Brush button; this is equivalent to single-clicking the brush and clicking on OK. (See Figure 6–3.)

 Tip of the paint brush defines the center of the current brush pattern.

Other than the fact that you can now paint multiple pixels at a time, the paint brush operates in exactly the same way as the Pencil tool. To paint in the current color, simply press the left mouse button and move the mouse. If the tip of the paint brush is on a pixel of any color other than the currently selected color when the mouse button is pressed down, then the paint brush will lay down colored pixels in the current color. If the tip of the paint brush is on a pixel of the current color when the mouse button is pressed, then the paint brush will act as an eraser, that is, the paint color will be white.

Click on one of these brush patterns to select the style of paint brush to use.

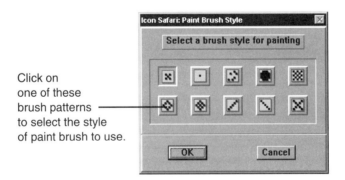

Figure 6–3 The Paint Brush Tool Options Dialog. You can select one of ten different brush styles for the paint brush using this dialog.

THE FILL TOOL (PAINT BUCKET)

Hint: The paint brush also has a built-in eraser which functions like the pencil's. To erase (paint in white) with the current brush style, click the paint brush on a pixel of the currently selected color.

Artist's Tip: To create dithered colors in the editing image, use one of the checkerboard brushes. Paint the basic pattern using the first color. Then use the Area Select tool and the Paint Bucket: Replace Fill tool to replace the white color with your second paint color.

THE FILL TOOL (PAINT BUCKET)

The Paint Bucket tool lets you fill pieces of your image with the currently selected color. By default, the paint bucket performs a *Flood Fill*. Click the tip of the Paint Bucket tool anywhere inside the area that you want filled; the Paint Bucket tool will perform a flood fill to the outer edges of that area. This feature works with any color area as the target, not just an empty (white) area. For example, if you have a solid blue circle, you can change it to green by selecting green from the color palette and then clicking the tip of the paint bucket anywhere in the circle. (See Figure 6–4.)

 Tip of the paint bucket defines the beginning pixel of the fill.

The paint bucket has another mode, *Replace Fill*. In this mode you can use the Paint Bucket to replace one color with another. (See Figure 6–5.) You can set the mode of the Paint Bucket tool by double-clicking on the Paint Bucket tool, or by selecting Set Paint Bucket from the Tools menu.

For example, using the Replace Fill mode, you could change all the light green pixels in your image into dark blue ones. To do so,

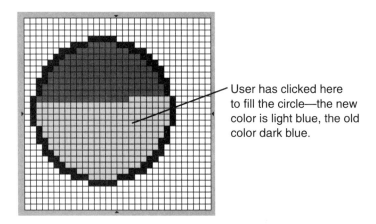

User has clicked here
to fill the circle—the new
color is light blue, the old
color dark blue.

Figure 6–4 An example of what happens when the user fills one color with another. It's possible to fill colors other than white.

When this button
is checked, the Paint
Bucket tool will perform
an ordinary flood fill.

When this button is checked,
the Paint Bucket tool will
perform a replace fill.

If this button is checked,
then the fill style selected
will be remembered for
future editing sessions.

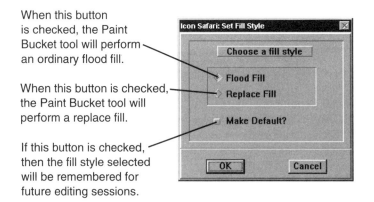

Figure 6–5 The Paint Bucket (Fill Tool) Control Dialog. This dialog lets you choose the two different types of behavior for the paint bucket—standard Flood Fill or magic mode Replace Fill.

1. Select dark blue from the color palette (click the tip of the paint bucket over the dark blue square).

2. Next, click the tip of the paint bucket on any light green pixel; all light green pixels will be instantly turned into dark blue ones.

Artist's Tip: Use the Replace Fill mode to erase small bits of image which are all the same color but not physically connected. Use the Area tool to select the area to erase and then use the Replace Fill with a drawing color of white.

THE SPRAY CAN TOOL

The Spray Can tool lets you spray paint pixels onto the Editing Grid, just the way a spray paint can would. The spray can has a set of 10 nozzles to choose from (the spray can nozzles have the same patterns as the brushes in the paint brush tool).

 Tip of spray can defines the center of the spray pattern.

In addition to different nozzle styles, you can also set the *nozzle flow* of the spray can. The nozzle flow controls how fast paint flows out of the spray can. It works the way a real spray paint can does—press lightly, and the spray can sprays just a little paint, slowly. Press heavily, and the spray can sprays a lot of paint, quickly.

You can select the nozzle style, and set the flow rate of the nozzle by selecting the Tools: Set Spray Can… menu entry, or by double-clicking on the Spray Can tool button. (See Figure 6–6 for the Spray Can dialog.)

In addition to selecting a nozzle, the spray paint can also has a Nozzle Flow control, which controls how much paint is sprayed out of the nozzle. The nozzle consists of a series of holes, and the spray rate defines how many of the holes in the nozzle must have paint go through them before the paint will stop flowing.

Select the nozzle pattern by clicking on one of the ten different patterns.

Define how fast paint flows through the nozzle here.

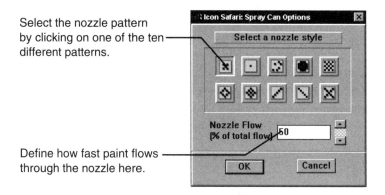

Figure 6–6 The Spray Can Options Dialog. You can control not only the nozzle pattern from here, but also how fast paint flows through that nozzle. The Nozzle Flow controls the amount of paint put through the nozzle each time you move the mouse—the higher the number, the more paint will flow through.

The nozzle flow rate ranges from 100% to –100%. At 100% all holes in the nozzle spray paint every time the mouse is moved. As the nozzle flow rate is decreased, fewer and fewer holes spray paint when the mouse moves, until at 0% none of the holes is spraying. Below 0% (i.e., negative percentages), the spray can acts like a vacuum and *sucks up* paint through the selected nozzle, in proportion to the chosen percentage. This means that you can selectively remove paint, through a particular nozzle pattern, by setting the flow rate as a negative number.

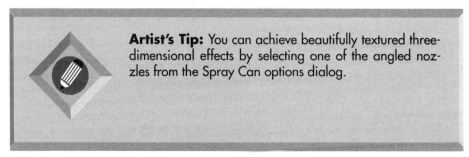

Artist's Tip: You can achieve beautifully textured three-dimensional effects by selecting one of the angled nozzles from the Spray Can options dialog.

Here's an example. We've selected the default nozzle (the far left nozzle in the upper row), and we've chosen a spray rate of 50%. What happens when we spray onto the grid?

Each time we move the mouse, the spray can must spray some paint through the holes in the nozzle. In our example, we've chosen a nozzle with 5 holes, so the spray can has to spray 50% of 5 holes, or 2.5 holes. Since paint cannot come out of half a hole, the end result is that sometimes 2 holes have paint pass through them, and sometimes 3 holes have paint pass through them, averaging out to 2.5 holes.

This means that the higher the nozzle flow, the more holes will have paint pass through them. At 100% nozzle flow, all the holes have paint pass through them, making the spray can the equivalent of the paint brush. At 0%, no holes will have paint pass through them. At –100%, paint will be removed through all the holes of the nozzle.

THE LINE TOOL

The Line tool lets you draw perfectly straight lines onto the Editing Grid. Once you've selected the Line Tool, you use it by pressing and *holding down* the left mouse button while in the Editing Grid. The first pixel that you click on becomes the starting point of your line. As long as you hold the left mouse button down, you can drag a "ghost line" around the screen. This line indicates the final placement of your line when you release the mouse button.

The ghost line lets you see where your line will be. Releasing the mouse button will draw the line in the current color.

Normally, the Line tool will erase (or undraw) a line if you start the line on a pixel of the currently selected color. (That is, the Line tool has a built-in eraser, the same way the Pencil tool does.) If you do not want the Line tool to behave this way, you can select the Set Line Tool entry from the Tools menu, or double-click on the Line tool, and bring up the Line Style dialog box (see Figure 6–7). If you check the button marked Always use selected color when drawing lines?, the Line tool will never erase but will always draw a line in the currently selected color.

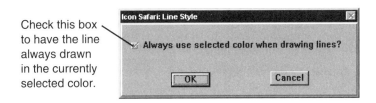

Check this box to have the line always drawn in the currently selected color.

Figure 6–7 The Line Style Dialog Box. You can turn the eraser behavior of the line on and off from this dialog box.

TO DRAW A LINE

1. Move the mouse cursor to the pixel where you want to start your line.

2. Press and hold down the left mouse button.

3. Drag the mouse around the editing area. A ghost line will follow the mouse cursor from your original starting point.

4. When the mouse cursor reaches the pixel where you want to end the line, release the mouse button. A line will be drawn between the starting and ending points in the currently selected color.

THE CIRCLE TOOL

The Circle tool lets you draw both perfect circles and ellipses onto the Editing Grid. Once you've selected the Circle tool, you use it by pressing and *holding down* the left mouse button while in the Editing Grid. The pixel that you click on first becomes the center of the circle. A dragable ghost circle will help you determine the size and placement of your circle. You may change the size of the ghost circle as long as you hold the left mouse button down.

Once you've chosen the size and position of your circle, release the mouse button. A circle is drawn around the initial pixel in the size you've selected, and in the current color.

To constrain the Circle tool to perfect circles, hold down the Shift key while dragging your circle.

Normally, the Circle tool will erase (or undraw) a line if you start the center of the circle on a pixel of the currently selected color. (That is, the Circle tool has a built-in eraser, the same way the Pencil tool does.) If you do not want the Circle tool to behave this way, you can select the Set Circle Tool entry from the Tools menu, or double-click on the Circle tool and bring up the Circle Style dialog box. (See Figure 6–8.) If you check the button marked Always use selected color when drawing circles?, the Circle tool will never erase but will always draw a circle in the currently selected color.

Check this box
to have the circle
always drawn
in the currently
selected color.

Figure 6–8 The Circle Style Dialog Box. You can turn the eraser behavior of the circle tool on and off from this dialog box.

TO DRAW AN ELLIPSE

1. Move the mouse cursor to the pixel where you want to start your ellipse. *This defines the center of the ellipse.*

2. Press and hold down the left mouse button.

3. Drag the mouse around the editing area. A ghost ellipse will follow the mouse cursor from your original starting point.

4. When the ellipse looks the way you want it to, release the mouse button. An ellipse will be drawn in the currently selected color.

TO DRAW A CIRCLE

1. Move the mouse cursor to the pixel where you want to start your circle. *This defines the center of the circle.*

2. Press and hold down the left mouse button. Also press and hold down the Shift key.

3. Drag the mouse around the editing area. A ghost circle will follow the mouse cursor from your original starting point.

4. When the circle looks the way you want it to, release the mouse button. A circle will be drawn in the currently selected color.

Artist's Tip: Smaller circles will appear less round and more blocky than bigger circles because the Circle tool has fewer pixels to work with when drawing smaller circles. For better looking circles, use a larger image area.

THE RECTANGLE TOOL

The Rectangle tool lets you draw rectangles onto the Editing Grid. Once you've selected the Rectangle tool, you use it by pressing and *holding down* the left mouse button while in the Editing Grid. The pixel that you first click on is the starting point of your rectangle. As long as you hold the left mouse button down, you can drag a ghost rectangle around the screen. This rectangle indicates the final size and shape of your rectangle should you release the mouse button.

Once you've chosen the size and shape of the rectangle, release the mouse button. The rectangle is drawn in your chosen position using the current color.

To constrain the Rectangle tool to draw perfect squares, hold down the Shift key while dragging the mouse.

Normally, the Rectangle tool will erase (or undraw) a rectangle if you start the corner of the rectangle on a pixel of the currently selected color. (That is, the Rectangle tool has a built-in eraser, the same way the Pencil tool does.) If you do not want the Rectangle tool to behave this way, you can select the Set Rectangle Tool entry from the Tools menu, or double-click on the Rectangle tool, and bring up the Rectangle Style dialog box. (See Figure 6–9.) If you check the button marked Always use selected color when drawing rectangles?, the Rectangle tool will never erase but will always draw a rectangle in the currently selected color.

DRAWING A RECTANGLE

1. Move the mouse cursor to the pixel where you want to start your rectangle. *This defines the corner of the rectangle.*

2. Press and hold down the left mouse button

Check this box
to have the rectangle
always drawn in the
currently selected ———
color.

Figure 6–9 The Rectangle Style Dialog Box. You can turn the eraser behavior of the rectangle tool on and off from this dialog box.

3. Drag the mouse around the editing area. A ghost rectangle will follow the mouse cursor from your original starting point.

4. When the rectangle is positioned where you want it to be, release the mouse button. A rectangle will be drawn in the currently selected color.

TO DRAW A SQUARE

1. Move the mouse cursor to the pixel where you want to start your square. *This defines the corner of the square.*

2. Press and hold down the left mouse button. Also press and hold down the Shift key.

3. Drag the mouse around the editing area. A ghost square will follow the mouse cursor from your original starting point.

4. When the square is positioned where you want it to be, release the mouse button. A square will be drawn in the currently selected color.

 **Artist's Tip:** You can block out an area for filling or changing by first drawing a rectangle in white around the area in question.

THE ARC TOOL

The Arc tool lets you create arcs (quarter sections of ellipses and circles) easily. Using the Arc tool is quite similar to using the Line tool. First, you select the starting point of the arc and mouse down. Then, while holding down the mouse, you move, and a ghost arc tracks your movement. When the arc is positioned the way you want it, you release the mouse button. If you hold down the Shift key while drawing, the arc will be constrained to a perfect section of a circle (quarter circle).

Normally, the Arc tool will erase (or undraw) an arc if you start the arc on a pixel of the currently selected color. (That is, the Arc tool has a built-in eraser, the same way the Pencil tool does.) If you do not want the Arc tool to behave this way, you can select the Set Arc Tool entry from the Tools menu, or double-click on the Arc tool and bring up the Arc Style dialog box. (See Figure 6–10.) If you check the button marked Always use selected color when drawing arcs?, the Arc tool will never erase, but will always draw an arc in the currently selected color.

Check this box to have the arc always drawn in the currently selected color.

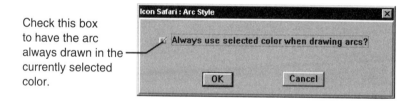

Figure 6–10 The Arc Style Dialog Box. You can turn the eraser behavior of the arc tool on and off from this dialog box.

TO DRAW AN ARC

1. Move the mouse cursor to the pixel where you want to start your arc.

2. Press and hold down the left mouse button.

3. Drag the mouse around the editing area. A ghost arc will follow the mouse cursor from your original starting point.

4. When the mouse cursor reaches the pixel where you want to end the arc, release the mouse button. An arc will be drawn between the starting and ending points in the currently selected color.

TO DRAW A PERFECTLY CIRCULAR ARC

1. Move the mouse cursor to the pixel where you want to start your arc.

2. Press and hold down the left mouse button. Also press and hold down the Shift key.

3. Drag the mouse around the editing area. A ghost arc will follow the mouse cursor from your original starting point.

4. When the mouse cursor reaches the pixel where you want to end the arc, release the mouse button. An arc will be drawn between the starting and ending points in the currently selected color.

THE MIRROR TOOL

The Mirror tool is the only tool of this group that does not directly create images. However, it controls the behavior of all the other image creation tools and so is grouped along with them.

The Mirror tool allows you to turn on a special drawing mode where each pixel that you draw is copied by the Icon Safari Editor to another part (or parts) of the Editing Grid. Depending upon the type of mirroring you have selected, pixels will be copied vertically, horizontally, or in different diagonal directions.

Normally, mirroring is turned off. However, when you single-click on the Mirror button, it depresses, indicating that mirroring is now on. You can press the button again to turn mirroring off.

To set up the types of mirroring that will occur when you draw, you can select the Set Mirror Tool entry from the Tools menu, or you can double-click on the mirroring tool itself. Either of these actions brings up the dialog box shown in Figure 6–11.

Figure 6–11 The Mirror Tool Dialog Box. This dialog allows you to define how mirroring works when turned on.

There are seven possible mirroring modes that you can choose. Each one reflects a point about an axis that is reflected with respect to the current point.

Each of the mirroring modes is independent of the others; you can choose one, several or all of the types of mirroring completely independently. (With all the different mirroring modes, there are an astonishing *5040* possible combinations of mirroring available to you!)

Each Mirror button controls mirroring for one of each of the seven octants that are empty when you are drawing (the eighth octant is the one that you're drawing in). By turning them on and off, you can begin to get a feel for how each type of mirroring works.

The Clear settings button allows you to turn off all the mirroring buttons at once.

The Make Default? box allows you to define the current mirroring mode as the one you want the Icon Safari Editor to come up in next time you run the program. By default, the Editor comes up with no forms of mirroring turned on.

Click on OK to choose the new mirroring style, or on Cancel to cancel the selection of a new style.

Mirroring affects all the drawing tools—Pencil, Paint Brush, Spray Can, Line, Circle, Rectangle, and Arc—with the exception of the Paint (Fill). The Paint Bucket is *not* mirrored. When mirroring is in effect, the drawing cursor will show a small mirror to the right of the cursor.

The following sketches show the cursors of the different drawing tools when mirroring is turned on.

 Draw cursor with mirroring on.

 Paint brush with mirroring on.

 Spray can with mirroring on.

 Select cursor (line, circle, rectangle) with mirroring on.

Image Manipulation Tools

The Icon Safari Editor has a highly sophisticated set of imaging tools; tools which will allow you to manipulate your image in an almost unlimited variety of ways. Some of the tools let you alter the way the current image looks; others define the way future imaging actions will take place. These tools are:

Full Clear	Clears the current image or selected portion
Invert (Yin-Yang)	Inverts the colors in the current image or selected portion
Shift	Shifts (moves) the image (or selected portion) in any of eight directions
Flip	Flips the image (or selected portion)
Rotate	Rotates the image (or selected portion)
Skew	Skews (bends) the image (or selected portion)
Area Select	Selects a portion of the image to work with
Mover	Grabs the selected portion of the image and moves it

Hint: With the exception of the Area Select tool itself, *all* of the image manipulation tools affect either the entire image, or if an area is selected, *only* the selected portion of the image.

FULL CLEAR

The Full Clear button will clear out (erase) the current image (or selected portion). If you are in Novice user mode, you will be cautioned about clearing the workspace; if you are in Expert User mode, the workspace will be cleared without warning.

TO CLEAR THE IMAGE

1. If you want to clear just a portion of the image, select the image with the Select tool.

2. Press the Full Clear button. The image is now cleared.

INVERT (YIN-YANG)

The Invert button (the one with the Yin-Yang symbol on it) will invert the colors in the current image (or selected portion). Each color is mapped to its inverse color; the inverse of a color is the color next to it (horizontally) in the Color Palette. Table 7–1 shows how colors are mapped to each other.

Table 7–1

Black	< - >	White
Dark Red	< - >	Light Blue
Dark Green	< - >	Pink
Brown	< - >	Royal Blue
Purple	< - >	Bright Yellow
Mauve	< - >	Bright Green
Steel Blue	< - >	Bright Red
Light Gray	< - >	Dark Gray

If you are in Novice user mode, you will be cautioned about performing this operation. In Expert user mode, the action will occur immediately.

TO INVERT THE IMAGE

1. If you want to invert just part of the image, select the portion of the image you want to invert using the Select tool.

2. Press the Invert button (Yin-Yang symbol). The image is now inverted.

SHIFT

The Shift dialog allows you to perform sophisticated shifts of the image (or selected portion). By typing a value into the shift box, you can shift the image more than 1 pixel at a time (in fact, you can shift the image up to 32 pixels at a time!) in any direction (shifting a large number of pixels takes proportionally longer than shifting a small number of pixels). You can also make the number of pixels shifted the default for future shift operations *from this dialog box*. The Fast Shift tool is unaffected by this number (Fast Shift buttons always shift a single pixel at a time). (See Figure 7–1.)

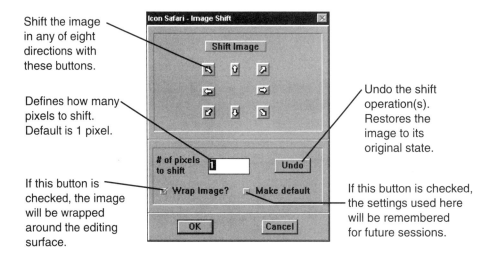

Shift the image in any of eight directions with these buttons.

Defines how many pixels to shift. Default is 1 pixel.

If this button is checked, the image will be wrapped around the editing surface.

Undo the shift operation(s). Restores the image to its original state.

If this button is checked, the settings used here will be remembered for future sessions.

Figure 7–1 The Shift Control Dialog Box. You can shift the image from this dialog box (as well as from the fast shift keys) and also control more sophisticated aspects of shifting.

Pressing each of the arrow buttons will move the image in the indicated direction. Undo will undo the last shift operation that you performed. The Make Default box, when checked, will make the # of pixels to shift the default for future operations. (The Icon Safari Editor will remember this number between sessions as well.)

The Wrap Image? box will toggle whether or not you want the Editor to wrap the pixels around the image when they hit an edge. When this button is checked, any pixel which hits the edge of the image will be brought around to the opposite side; thus, if a pixel is shifted off the top of the image, it will be brought around to the bottom and put back on. If the Wrap Image? box is *not* checked, then any pixel which reaches the edge falls off and is lost.

TO SHIFT THE IMAGE 2 PIXELS AT A TIME

1. Click on the exclamation mark button in the middle of the fast shift tools. The shift dialog is brought up.

2. Select the edit box next to # of pixels to shift. Enter a 2.

3. Click on the arrow button in the direction you want to shift.

FLIP

Flip allows you to flip the image (or selected portion) either vertically or horizontally. When you flip the image, the pixels in the image are swapped end for end. For example, if you flip the entire image horizontally, the left side of the image becomes the right side and the right side becomes the left side.

Click on the Horizontal button to flip the image horizontally, and on the Vertical button to flip it vertically.

TO FLIP THE IMAGE HORIZONTALLY (LEFT TO RIGHT)

1. If you want to flip just part of the image, select the portion of the image you want to flip using the Select tool.

2. Press the Horizontal Shift button—the one with the image and arrow flipping from left to right. The image is now flipped horizontally.

TO FLIP THE IMAGE
VERTICALLY (TOP TO BOTTOM)

1. If you want to flip just part of the image, select the portion of the image you want to flip using the Select tool.

2. Press the Vertical Shift button—the one with the image and arrow flipping from top to bottom. The image is now flipped vertically.

ROTATE

Rotate allows you to rotate the image (or a selected portion) in one of four directions, either to the left 180 degrees, to the left 90 degrees, to the right 90 degrees, or to the right 180 degrees.

Click on the button corresponding to the direction you want to rotate the image.

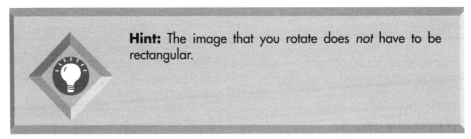

Hint: The image that you rotate does *not* have to be rectangular.

SKEW

Skewing an image is a process that allows you to *bend* the image (or currently selected portion) in a given direction by a certain amount. The default skews are set for a 45-degree angle, left, right, up and down, but you can perform more sophisticated skewing actions by selecting the Exclamation Mark button just to the left of the skew tools. (See Figure 7–2.) This brings up the Skew Tool dialog (which can also be brought up by selecting the Skew Tool entry from the Tools menu).

How drastically the image is bent is controlled by the *skew angle*, which you set with the two angle edit controls, and the vertical and horizontal scrollers. The higher the angle (up to a maximum of ±90 degrees), the greater the amount of skew that is applied.

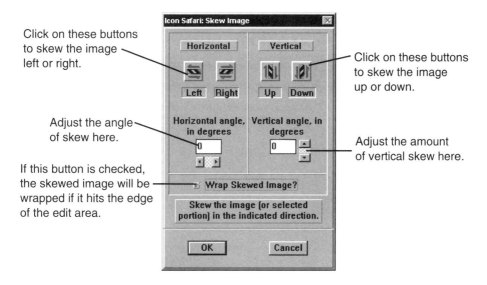

Click on these buttons
to skew the image
left or right.

Click on these buttons
to skew the image
up or down.

Adjust the angle
of skew here.

Adjust the amount
of vertical skew here.

If this button is checked,
the skewed image will be
wrapped if it hits the edge
of the edit area.

Figure 7–2 The Skew Tool Control Dialog. You can skew the image from here, and also control the amount of skew that the skew controls will use. The skew controls on the main menu always skew at a 45-degree angle.

Once you've chosen a skew angle, you can skew the image using the four skew buttons. For example, to skew the image left by 45 degrees, you would:

1. Enter 45 into the horizontal angle edit control, either by typing in the value 45, or by using the scroller arrows;

2. Press the Left Skew button.

Pressing the Right Skew button would skew the image to the right by 45 degrees (in our example, pressing the Right Skew button would undo the effects of the Left Skew button).

Hint: Entering a negative skew angle and pressing one of the skew buttons has the same effect as entering a positive skew angle and pressing the opposite button. For example, entering –20 and pressing Up Skew results in the same thing as entering 20 and pressing Down Skew.

TO SKEW AN IMAGE 45 DEGREES TO THE LEFT

1. Select the portion of the image you want to skew using the select tool. If you want to skew the entire image, do not select anything.

2. Click on the Left Skew button. The image is now skewed to the left 45 degrees.

AREA SELECT TOOL

The Area Select tool allows you to specify a piece of the image that subsequent Image Manipulation Tool operations will act on (such as flipping or shifting). Most graphic operations either operate on the entire image, or on the selected portion of it. The area that you select is known as the Currently selected area.

To select an area, click above and to the left of the corner of the pixel that you want; drag the ghost box down and to the right, making sure to *fully* enclose the area that you want to select. Once you release the mouse button, the ghost box will snap inwards to the nearest fully enclosed area.

To cancel an area selection, click on one of the image creation tools (Pencil, Paint Brush, Spray Can, and so on), or click outside the Editing Grid.

Hint: To help you better position your selection area, you can view the mouse cursor's coordinates by choosing the Show Mouse Position entry on the Options menu. This will allow you to more precisely place your selection.

MOVER TOOL

In order to use the Mover tool you must have first selected an area (see Area Select Tool). Once you have an area selected, you can use the Mover tool to drag it around the edit area. Simply click and hold down the mouse button anywhere inside the selected area. A ghost box will appear in the same size and shape as the selected area. Drag this ghost box to the point where you want the image to be; then release the mouse button. The image will be moved to the new position.

You can control the behavior of the Mover tool through the Mover Tool dialog box. To bring up this dialog, double-click on the Mover tool, or select the Mover Tool entry from the Tools menu. The dialog is shown in Figure 7–3.

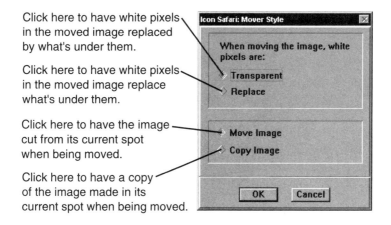

Click here to have white pixels in the moved image replaced by what's under them.

Click here to have white pixels in the moved image replace what's under them.

Click here to have the image cut from its current spot when being moved.

Click here to have a copy of the image made in its current spot when being moved.

Figure 7–3 The Mover Tool Control Panel. You can have the Mover tool either move an image or copy it. You can also define for the Mover tool how white pixels are treated when moving an image.

If you have Erase Original Image? checked in the Style: Mover Style menu, then the original image will be erased before the new image is moved. If this entry is not checked, then a *copy* of the image will be put at the new location, and the original image will remain untouched.

Hint: Moving the image does *not* undo the selected area. This means you can move an image several times without reselecting the image each time.

Artist's Tip: By turning off the Erase Original Image? flag (see Style: Mover Style menu), you can make multiple overlapping copies of an image, and achieve a staggered or 3D look.

8

The Icon Safari Editor Menus

The Icon Safari Editor has seven menus. They are

File	File commands
Edit	Editing commands
Tool	Control of the Editing tools
Options	Options and controls
Icon	Icon-specific commands
Cursor	Cursor-specific commands
Help	On-line help for Icon Safari

For information about each menu and its entries, please turn to the relevant section.

THE FILE MENU

Under the Icon Safari Editor's FILE menu, you'll find the following entries:

New	Creates a new image
Open...	Opens a current image file
Save	Saves the image to the current file
Save As...	Saves the current image to a different file
Snapshot	Grabs an image from the screen
Open Library...	Opens an icon library
Icon Library...	Goes to the icon library manager
Exit	Exits the Editor.

These menu entries are described in detail on the following pages. See Figure 8–1 for the menu entries.

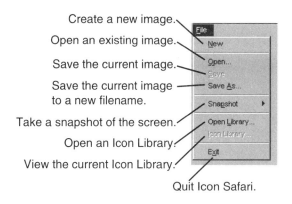

Create a new image.
Open an existing image.
Save the current image.
Save the current image
to a new filename.
Take a snapshot of the screen.
Open an Icon Library.
View the current Icon Library.
Quit Icon Safari.

Figure 8–1 The File Menu of the Icon Safari Editor.

File: New

The New menu entry allows you to create a new image of the currently selected type (see Options: Image Type for more information about setting the image type). It clears out any current work that you have and sets appropriate defaults based on your selected image type. New also clears any file name that may be in use.

Note: If you have an animation loaded, or in progress, the New command will clear the animation.

Hint: You should always use the New menu entry to create a new image when you have finished editing your current one. Simply pressing the Full Clear button, although it will *erase* your image, will not clear out the filename, or set up any of the other appropriate defaults for a new image. Be careful, or you could end up saving your new image into the old filename, destroying your old image in the process. Using the New menu will avoid this danger.

File: Open

The Open command allows you to open a file that has been previously saved to disk. You can open one of four file types:

*.ICO, for icon images stored in standard format,
*.CUR, for cursor images,
*.BMP, for bitmap images, and
*.ANI for cursor and icon animations.

Selecting the Open command brings up the dialog shown in Figure 8–2. You can select one of the four different file formats by choosing the type under the List files of Type drop-down box. Choosing the file type also selects the actual image type that you will be working with; thus, if you load an ICO file, the image type will be set to Icon. The exception to this are animations, which derive their type from the basic image type that they are based on (i.e., a cursor animation is treated as a series of cursors, etc.).

> **CAUTION!** Do *NOT* attempt to load a different type of image file by typing into the filename box something such as "*.ICO" when you have the bitmap type selected. Doing so will yield unpredictable results, since you are telling the Editor that you are loading both an icon image and a bitmap image at the same time.

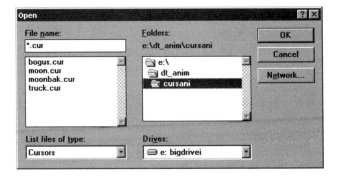

Figure 8–2 The File Open dialog box that comes up when you open a file in the Editor. This is the standard Windows File Open dialog.

File: Save

The Save command saves your current image in its current file. If you have created a new image using the New command, you will need to use the Save As... command first in order to create a filename for the image.

You will always be prompted by the alert box Overwrite current file?. You can click on Yes to save the file, or No to cancel the operation.

Hint: The Save command is only turned on when you have made changes to your work. If you have not made any changes to the image since you last saved it, or if the image does not yet have a filename, then the Save menu is grayed out.

File: Save As

The Save As... command allows you to save your current image to disk under another filename. It also allows you to change the type of image that you are going to save. By selecting one of the file types from the Save File as Type: drop-down list box (see Figure 8–3)—*.ICO, for cursor images, *.BMP for bitmap images, *.CUR for cursor images, *.ANI for animations—you are selecting not only the file extension of the file, but its format as well. This means that you can easily change a cursor image to a bitmap image just by changing the radio button setting.

Hint: Due to differences in file formats, it is not always possible to save an image into a different format. When this happens, the Icon Safari Editor will alert you to the situation and request that you make the necessary modifications to allow the image to be saved in the requested format.

For example, cursors are monochrome images and use only black and white (as well as two special colors, clear and inverse). If you attempt to save a cursor image that uses more than these four colors, the Editor will alert you with a message telling you that you must change all incorrect colors before you can save the file.

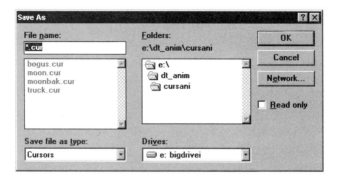

Figure 8–3 The standard File Save As dialog box that comes up when you select the Save As… entry from the File menu.

File: Snapshot

The Snapshot tool provides a way of obtaining images (primarily icon images) that the Icon Safari Editor cannot extract in any other fashion. Given that the Editor understands a wide variety of file formats and resources, this may not happen very often. Although some programs do not store icon images directly, you can still get a copy of the icon image associated with such files by using the Snapshot tool.

The Fixed Size will grab a fixed 32x32 image from any portion of the screen.

USING SNAPSHOT-FIXED SIZE

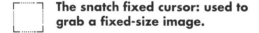 **The snatch fixed cursor: used to grab a fixed-size image.**

1. Iconify the Icon Safari Editor. (Press the down arrow in the upper-right corner of the Icon Safari Editor main window.)

2. Make sure that the icon image you want to Snapshot is visible somewhere on the screen. (Anywhere is fine, just as long as the entire image is clear and unobstructed.)

3. De-iconify the Icon Safari Editor and select Snapshot-Fixed Size from the File menu. At this point the Editor iconifies itself and displays the Snapshot cursor, which is a rectangular box,

32 pixels high and 32 pixels wide. Position the Snapshot cursor over the image you wish to capture and click the left mouse button. The image will be transferred to the Editor's Editing Grid area, ready for manipulation.

Hint: The Snapshot tool is not restricted to icon images displayed on screen; virtually any portion of the visible screen can be snatched. However, the Snapshot tool is limited to snatching physical palette colors only. As a result, if you attempt to snatch a portion of the screen display which is using a dithered pattern to represent a color, then you will get the message: "Cannot get matching color for pixel"; any pixels which are found which cannot be matched will be set to white.

File: Open Library

The Open Library menu entry allows you to import compiled icon and cursor resource images directly from a number of different file formats. Icons and cursors can exist in any of the following file formats (although a given file of a given type may not contain either kind of image):

.EXE—standard Windows executable files
.DLL—standard Windows dynamic link libraries (not all DLL's
        contain icons and/or cursors)
.DRV—Windows driver files
.IL—HDC Icon Library files

After you select the file to import, the Icon Safari Editor will check the file to see if there are any icon or cursor images in it; if there are, the Editor will load them into the Icon Library Manager and automatically bring up the Library Manager, so that you can see and manipulate the images.

For more information on using the Icon Library Manager, see File: Icon Library.

File: Icon Library

The Icon Library menu entry will bring up the Icon Library Manager window; this is the window where you perform all manipulations on icon libraries. If you have an Icon Library currently loaded, then you will see the icon images that it contains displayed in the Icon Library window; otherwise you will see 15 spaces, each bearing the legend Empty below it. (See Figure 8–4.)

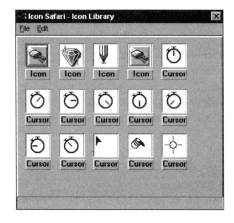

Figure 8–4 The Icon Safari Icon Library control. You can view icons, cursors and bitmaps in different files using this tool.

To edit one of the icons or cursors, double-click on that icon. To move around in the Icon Library Manager, use the scroll and arrow keys. You can replace any icon or cursor in an existing icon library by selecting the icon or cursor that you wish to replace and then selecting Edit: Replace from the Edit menu. The selected icon or cursor will be replaced with the current edit image.

Once you've changed some of the images, you can save the file to disk by using Save… . The images will not be changed until you save them. Just changing them in the Icon Library Manager will *not* change them in the file.

The Icon Library Manager is one of the most powerful features of Icon Safari Editor. By having the Library Manager integrated directly with the editing tools, you can easily move images from one area to the other with just a few mouse clicks. Because the Icon Library Manager can read from and write to so many different kinds of file formats, it extends your image management capabilities more fully than other separate programs.

The Icon Library Manager has its own menu set; the commands on these menus allow you to control the Library Manager.

The *File* commands are used to open, save and export icon image files, as well as query the current library regarding the number of icon images, groups and cursors that it contains.

The *Edit* commands are used to edit, replace and clear an icon or cursor image in the current library.

Hint: The Icon Library Manager makes no distinction between .EXE files and .DLL files. This means that you can also change the icon and cursor images that get used by some systemwide programs.

Artist's Tip: One feature of the Library Manager that many people find particularly useful is its ability to intelligently replace only those images in a file which have changed. This means that you can replace just one icon in an .exe file, for example, without changing (or worrying about) any other portion of the file.

For example, if you wish to change the icon associated with the Windows program FOO, you would use the Open Library command from the main editing window, or open FOO from the Icon Library Manager. The Icon Safari Editor would then load all icons and cursors that it found in FOO. You could now double-click on the icon or cursor image that you wanted to edit and then replace it when you have finished. Alternatively, you could simply insert an entirely new icon or cursor image into the spot where one already existed. Once you had finished, you would save the file (using the File: Save command from the Icon Library Manager menu). The Editor would export *only* that image to the file, and no other; this means that the update of the file occurs much faster than if the whole file had to be rewritten.

 **Hint:** When replacing an icon image in a currently existing file, make sure that the number of colors, height and width all match, or you'll receive the message that one of those elements is mismatched. All the elements must match in order to correctly replace the image in the file.

File: Exit

The Exit file exits the Icon Safari Editor. All default settings that you have requested during the editing session will be saved to disk for next time.

   If you haven't saved your current work, and you are in Novice mode, then you will be warned; otherwise, the Editor will exit immediately.

THE EDIT MENU

The Edit menu contains entries which deal with the Undo buffers (the Icon Safari Editor has five undo buffers, stacked from most recently used to least recently used), and cutting, copying and pasting from both the clipboard and the Editor's internal buffer. See Figure 8–5 for the Edit menus.

Undo Last	Undoes the last operation
Undo...	Selects the image to undo
Cut To Clipboard	Cuts image to the Windows Clipboard
Copy To Clipboard	Copies the image to the Windows Clipboard
Paste From Clipboard	Pastes from the Windows Clipboard
Cut To Buffer	Cuts to the Editor's buffer
Copy To Buffer	Copies to the Editor's buffer
Paste From Buffer	Pastes from the Editor's buffer

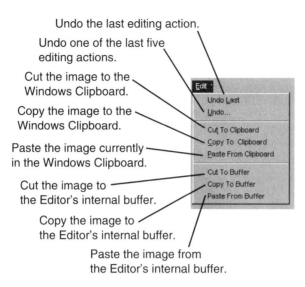

Undo the last editing action.

Undo one of the last five editing actions.

Cut the image to the Windows Clipboard.

Copy the image to the Windows Clipboard.

Paste the image currently in the Windows Clipboard.

Cut the image to the Editor's internal buffer.

Copy the image to the Editor's internal buffer.

Paste the image from the Editor's internal buffer.

Figure 8–5 The Edit Menu of the Icon Safari Editor.

The Icon Safari Editor supports cutting and pasting from two different areas—one is the *standard Windows Clipboard*, which the Editor communicates with using the device dependent bitmap format.

The Icon Safari Editor also supports cutting and pasting to a special *internal buffer*, which is entirely separate from the clipboard. The internal buffer not only supports cutting and copying of the full image, but also supports cutting and pasting *pieces* of the image. What this means is that you can cut or copy two different pieces of your image to the two different buffers and then paste them back together with a third piece, almost instantly.

Artist's Tip: If you do a lot of cutting and pasting of images, we suggest that you try using both buffers, instead of merely relying on one or the other. We think you'll find that you not only save a great deal of time, but that you also gain a great deal of additional flexibility.

Edit: Undo Last

Undo Last immediately undoes the last operation performed.

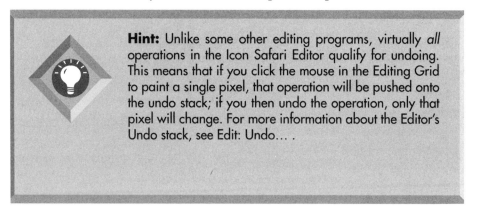

Hint: Unlike some other editing programs, virtually *all* operations in the Icon Safari Editor qualify for undoing. This means that if you click the mouse in the Editing Grid to paint a single pixel, that operation will be pushed onto the undo stack; if you then undo the operation, only that pixel will change. For more information about the Editor's Undo stack, see Edit: Undo... .

Edit: Undo

Most Windows programs have a limited Undo capability; usually, you can undo only the last operation that you performed. The Icon Safari Editor, however, has a more sophisticated capability—it remembers not just the last operation that you performed, but also the last *five operations*. It keeps track of the last five versions of your image on an Undo stack. This stack is a push-down stack; that is, whenever you complete your current imaging operation (for example, you lift off the mouse button to finish a paint operation), the Editor takes the current image and pushes it onto the Undo stack. The four images below it are pushed down, and the image on the bottom of the Undo stack falls off and is lost.

The Undo command is somewhat different than Undo Last, in that it presents you with a small dialog box in which are displayed the last five images that were worked on, in sequential order from right to left (that is, the oldest image is on the far right, and the most recent image is on the far left). (See Figure 8–6.)

To undo to one of these images, simply double-click on the desired image.

To abort the Undo process, click on Cancel.

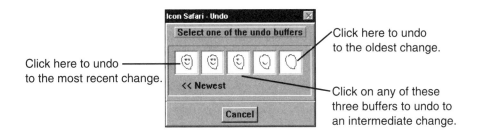

Click here to undo to the most recent change.

Click here to undo to the oldest change.

Click on any of these three buffers to undo to an intermediate change.

Figure 8-6 The Icon Safari Editor's Undo Buffer. Not only can you undo to any of the last five editing actions, but you can also visually distinguish which edit you wish to return to.

Edit: Cut To Clipboard

This operation cuts the image currently in the edit area to the Windows clipboard in bitmap format. In the cut operation, a copy of the current image is put into the clipboard, and then the Editing Grid is cleared.

Artist's Tip: If you want to retain your image after you put it into the clipboard, don't use the Cut To Clipboard command; use Copy To Clipboard instead. Copying (see Copy To Clipboard) an image is identical to cutting an image, except that the image is not cleared after a copy is put into the clipboard.

Hint: The currently selected area (if there is one) does not affect the image which gets cut to the clipboard. That is, the *entire image* is always cut to the clipboard, whether or not you currently have an image selected.

Edit: Copy to clipboard

This function copies the current edit image to the Windows Clipboard in bitmap format. Unlike cutting (see Cut To Clipboard), copying does *not* clear the Editing Grid after the operation has occurred.

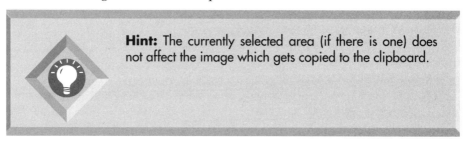

Hint: The currently selected area (if there is one) does not affect the image which gets copied to the clipboard.

Edit: Paste From clipboard

This function copies the current contents of the clipboard (if available in bitmap format) into the editing area.

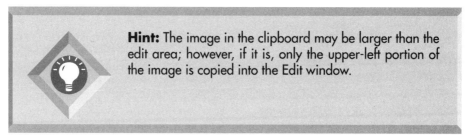

Hint: The image in the clipboard may be larger than the edit area; however, if it is, only the upper-left portion of the image is copied into the Edit window.

Edit: Cut To Buffer

Cut To Buffer cuts the current editing image (or selected portion) to the Editor's internal image buffer and erases that portion of it from the editing area. This buffer is separate from the clipboard and is unaffected by it. Furthermore, the internal image buffer can hold either the entire editing image, or, if there is a selected area, it will cut only that portion of the image.

Hint: If you have an area selected, then *only* that piece of the image will be copied to the internal buffer of the Editor. The rest of the image will *not* be copied. If you cut a portion of the image, the Editor will remember the position from which you cut it.

Edit: Copy To Buffer

This function copies the current edit image (or selected portion) to the Editor's internal image buffer and leaves the current image intact.

The internal image buffer is separate from and unaffected by the Windows Clipboard.

See also Cut To Buffer.

Hint: If you have an area selected, then *only* that piece of the image will be copied to the internal buffer of the Editor. The rest of the image will *not* be copied.

Edit: Paste From Buffer

Paste From Buffer pastes the image out of the Icon Safari Editor's internal buffer into the editing area.

If the image that was cut/copied was a selected portion of the image, then it will be pasted back into the same place. For example, if you cut a portion of an image starting at pixel (2,2) and ending at pixel (20,20), then when you paste that image back in, the image will be placed with its upper-left corner starting at (2,2), and end with the lower-right corner placed at (20,20).

THE TOOLS MENU

The Tools menu of the Icon Safari Editor allows you to control the settings of all of the different tools in the Editor. It has 13 entries. (See Figure 8–7.)

Set Pencil Tool...	Sets the properties of the Pencil tool
Set Paint Brush...	Sets the properties of the Paint Brush tool
Set Spray Can...	Sets the properties of the Spray Can tool
Set Paint Bucket...	Sets the properties of the Paint Bucket tool
Set Eraser...	Sets the properties of the Eraser tool
Set Line Tool...	Sets the properties of the Line tool
Set Circle Tool...	Sets the properties of the Circle tool
Set Rectangle Tool...	Sets the properties of the Rectangle tool
Set Arc Tool...	Sets the properties of the Arc tool
Set Mover Tool...	Sets the properties of the Mover tool
Set Mirror Tool...	Sets the properties of the Mirror tool
Shift Tool...	Sets the properties of the Shift tool
Skew Tool...	Sets the properties of the Skew tool

Tools: Set Pencil Tool

This entry brings up the Pencil Tool settings dialog (see Figure 8–8). This dialog allows you to control the eraser behavior of the Pencil tool.

If the Always use selected color? box is *not* checked, it means that the Icon Safari Editor considers the color of the pixel at the starting point of whatever you draw.

If the pixel at the starting point is the same color as the current drawing color, then the Editor will draw the new line in white. For example, if the current drawing color is light blue and you start on a pixel that is light blue, the Editor will draw the new pixels in white—essentially, it will undraw whatever is in the Editing Grid.

Figure 8–7 The Tools Menu of the Icon Safari Editor.

If the pixel at the starting point is not the same color as the current drawing color, the Editor draws the line in the current drawing color. For example, if the currently selected color is light blue and you start a line on a pixel that is dark green, then the line will be drawn in light blue. If you start a line on a pixel that is light blue already, then the line is drawn in white (i.e., erased).

If the Always use selected color? box is checked, the Editor will always draw in the currently selected color.

Tools: Set Paint Brush

This option brings up the dialog box which lets you choose the brush that will be used for future paint operations. (See Figure 8–9.)

To select one of the brushes, first single-click on the Brush button and then on OK. You can also select a brush by double-clicking on the Brush button; this is equivalent to single-clicking the Brush button and clicking on OK.

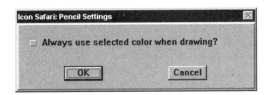

Figure 8–8 The Pencil Tool Settings Dialog Box.

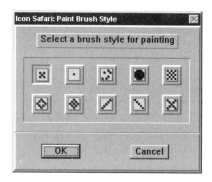

Figure 8–9 The Paint Brush Settings Dialog Box.

Artist's Tip: The paint brush works in the same fashion as the Pencil tool. If the tip of the paint brush is on a pixel of any color other than the currently selected color when the mouse button is pressed down, then the paint brush will lay down colored pixels in the current color. If the tip of the paint brush is on a pixel of the current color when the mouse button is pressed, then the paint brush will act as an eraser; that is, the paint color will be white.

Tools: Set Spray Can

This option brings up the dialog box which lets you choose the nozzle that will be used for future paint operations. (See Figure 8–10.)

In addition to selecting a nozzle, the spray paint can also has a Nozzle Flow control, which controls how much paint is sprayed out of the nozzle. The nozzle consists of a series of holes, and the spray rate defines how many of the holes in the nozzle must have paint go through them before the paint will stop flowing.

Here's an example. We've selected the default nozzle (the far-left nozzle in the upper row), and we've chosen a spray rate of 50%. What happens when we spray onto the grid?

Each time we move the mouse, the spray can must spray some paint through the holes in the nozzle. In our example, we've chosen a nozzle with 5 holes, so the spray can has to spray 50% of 5 holes, or 2.5 holes. Since paint cannot come out of half a hole, the end result is that some-

Figure 8-10 The Spray Can Settings Dialog Box.

times 2 holes have paint pass through them, and sometimes 3 holes have paint pass through them, averaging out to 2.5 holes.

This means that the higher the nozzle flow, the more holes will have paint pass through them. At 100% nozzle flow, all the holes have paint pass through them, making the spray can the equivalent of the paint brush. At 0%, no holes will have paint pass through them.

Artist's Tip: The nozzle flow can also be adjusted to *negative* numbers. When this is done, the spray can acts as a vacuum cleaner—instead of spraying paint down, it sucks it up, off of the editing grid. You can use this feature to create images with a fragmented look.

Tools: Set Paint Bucket

When you select this menu entry, the Paint Bucket options dialog box is brought up. (See Figure 8–11.) The paint can has two options, Flood Fill and Replace Fill.

Figure 8-11 The Paint Bucket (Fill Tool) Settings Dialog Box.

When Icon Safari Editor is run for the first time, Flood Fill is the default mode. In this mode, the paint can will perform a flood fill outwards from the selected pixel.

 Tip of the paint bucket defines the beginning pixel of the fill.

Replace Fill is also known as magic mode. In magic mode, when you click on a pixel in the Editing Grid, all pixels of that color are replaced by the current palette color. For example, if the current paint color is dark blue and you click on a light green pixel in the Editing Grid, then all light green pixels are turned into dark blue ones. Magic!

The Make Default? check box allows you to make the current fill style the default. When checked, the current fill style will be saved to disk. The next time you run the Editor this fill style will automatically be selected at startup. If you want the fill style to apply only to this editing session, do not check this box.

Tools: Set Eraser

This menu entry brings up the Eraser Settings dialog box. (See Figure 8–12.) From here you can set the size of the eraser, as well as its behavior.

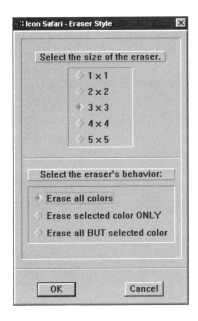

Figure 8–12 The Eraser Tool Settings Dialog Box.

The eraser is always a square and its size can be set from a square 1x1 (that is, a single pixel) to a square 5x5 (five pixels on a side, or a total of 25 pixels). Click on the radio button next to the size you want.

The eraser also can have one of three types of behavior associated with it.

Erase all colors	Erases all colors in the Editing Grid
Erase selected color ONLY	Erases *only* pixels of the currently selected color
Erase all BUT selected color	Erases all pixels *except* those of the currently selected color.

Tools: Set Line Tool

The Set Line Tool menu controls how lines are drawn by Icon Safari Editor. Selecting it brings up the Line Tool Settings dialog box (see Figure 8–13).

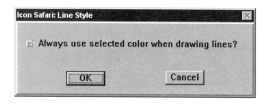

Figure 8-13 The Line Tool Settings Dialog Box.

If the box Always use selected color when drawing lines? is *not* selected, it means that the Icon Safari Editor considers the color of the pixel at the starting point of any line that you draw.

If the pixel at the starting point of a line is the same color as the current drawing color, then the Editor will draw the new line in white. For example, if the current drawing color is light blue and you start a line on a pixel that is light blue, the Editor will draw the new line in white—essentially, it will undraw the line.

If the pixel at the starting point of a line is not the same color as the current drawing color, the Editor draws the line in the current drawing color. For example, if the currently selected color is light blue and you start a line on a pixel that is dark green, then the line will be drawn in light blue. If you start a line on a pixel that is light blue already, then the line is drawn in white (i.e., erased).

Hint: By leaving the Always use selected color when drawing lines? button unchecked, you can ensure accurate placement of lines. If a line doesn't come out correctly, draw it again, using the same exact starting and ending points, and the line will be erased.

If you select Always use selected color when drawing lines?, the Editor will always draw lines in the currently selected color.

Tools: Set Circle Tool

The Set Circle Tool menu controls how circles are drawn by Icon Safari Editor. Selecting it brings up the Circle Tool Settings dialog box (see Figure 8–14).

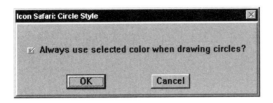

Figure 8–14 The Circle Tool Settings Dialog Box.

If the box Always use selected color when drawing circles? is *not* selected, it means that the Icon Safari Editor considers the color of the pixel at the starting point of any circle that you draw.

If the pixel at the starting point of a circle is the same color as the current drawing color, then the Editor will draw the new circle in white. For example, if the current drawing color is light blue and you start a circle on a pixel that is light blue, the Editor will draw the new circle in white—essentially, it will undraw the circle. If you start a circle on a pixel that is a different color, the Editor will draw the circle in light blue.

If the pixel at the starting point of a circle is not the same color as the current drawing color, the Editor draws the circle in the current drawing color.

If you select Always use selected color when drawing circles?, the Editor will always draw circles in the currently selected color.

Tools: Set Rectangle Tool

The Set Rectangle Tool menu controls how rectangles are drawn by Icon Safari Editor. Selecting it brings up the Rectangle Tool Settings dialog box (see Figure 8–15).

If the box Always use selected color when drawing rectangles? is *not* selected, it means that the Icon Safari Editor considers the color of the pixel at the starting point of any rectangle that you draw.

If the pixel at the starting point of a rectangle is the same color as the current drawing color, then the Editor will draw the new rectangle in white. For example, if the current drawing color is light blue and you

Figure 8–15 The Rectangle Tool Settings Dialog Box.

start a rectangle on a pixel that is light blue, the Editor will draw the new rectangle in white—essentially, it will undraw the rectangle. If you start a rectangle on a pixel that is a different color, the Editor will draw the rectangle in light blue.

If the pixel at the starting point of a rectangle is not the same color as the current drawing color, the Editor draws the rectangle in the current drawing color.

If you select Always use selected color when drawing rectangles?, the Editor will always draw rectangles in the currently selected color.

Tools: Set Arc Tool

The Set Arc Tool menu controls how arcs are drawn by Icon Safari Editor. Selecting it brings up the Arc Tool Settings dialog box (see Figure 8–16).

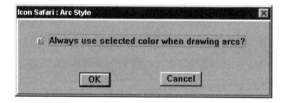

Figure 8–16 The Arc Tool Settings Dialog Box.

If the box Always use selected color when drawing arcs? is *not* selected, it means that the Icon Safari Editor considers the color of the pixel at the starting point of any arc that you draw.

If the pixel at the starting point of a arc is the same color as the current drawing color, then the Editor will draw the new arc in white. For example, if the current drawing color is light blue and you start a arc on a pixel that is light blue, the Editor will draw the new arc in white—essentially, it will undraw the arc. If you start a arc on a pixel that is a different color, the Editor will draw the arc in light blue.

If the pixel at the starting point of a arc is not the same color as the current drawing color, the Editor draws the arc in the current drawing color.

If you select Always use selected color when drawing arcs?, the Editor will always draw arcs in the currently selected color.

Tools: Set Mover Tool

The Set Mover Tool menu controls how the Editor treats images which are moved using the Mover tool (see Mover Tool for more information). When you select it, it brings up the Mover Tool Settings dialog (see Figure 8–17).

Figure 8–17 The Mover Tool Settings Dialog Box.

The first two entries control how the moved image is laid down onto the new area of the edit window. If Transparent is selected, then any pixel which is white in the selected area *does not* replace any underlying pixel; if Replace is selected, then white pixels do replace underlying colored pixels.

The second two entries—Move image or Copy image—control whether the Mover tool functions as a Move or a Copy.

If the Move entry is selected, then the tool acts as a Move tool and deletes the moved image from the original position.

If the Copy entry is selected, then the Move tool performs a copy of the original image into the new spot and leaves the original image unchanged. In areas where the new image overlaps the original image, the new image is retained.

Tools: Set Mirror Tool

The Set Mirror Tool menu entry brings up the Mirroring Tool Settings dialog (see Figure 8–18). You can control how mirroring is performed with this dialog box.

Figure 8–18 The Mirror Tool Settings Dialog Box.

There are seven possible mirroring modes that you can choose. Each one reflects a point about an axis that is reflected with respect to the current point.

Each of the mirroring modes is independent of the others; you can choose one, several or all of the types of mirroring, completely independently. (With all the different mirroring modes, there are an astonishing *5040* possible combinations of mirroring available to you!)

Each mirror button controls mirroring for one of each of the seven octants that are empty when you are drawing (the eighth octant is the one that you're drawing in). By turning them on and off, you can begin to get a feel for how each type of mirroring works.

The Clear Settings button allows you to turn off all the mirroring buttons at once.

The Make Default? box allows you to define the current mirroring mode as the one you want the Icon Safari Editor to come up in next time you run the program. By default, the Editor comes up with no forms of mirroring turned on.

Tools: Shift Tool

Selecting the Shift Tool menu entry brings up the Shift Tool dialog box, which allows you to perform sophisticated shifts of the image (or a selected portion of it). (See Figure 8–19.) By typing a value into the shift box, you can shift the image more than 1 pixel at a time (in fact, you can shift the image up to 32 pixels at a time!) in any direction. (Shifting a large number of pixels takes proportionally longer than shifting a small number of pixels.) You can also make the number of pixels shifted the default for future shift operations *from this dialog box*. The Fast Shift tool is unaffected by this number (Fast Shift buttons always shift a single pixel at a time).

Pressing each of the arrow buttons will move the image in the indicated direction. Undo will undo the last shift operation that you performed. The Make default box, when checked, will make the # of pixels to shift the default for future operations. (Icon Safari will remember this number between sessions as well.)

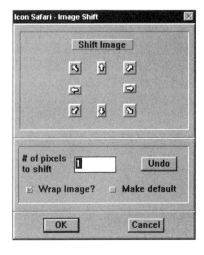

Figure 8–19 The Shift Tool Settings Dialog Box.

The Wrap image? box will toggle whether or not you want Icon Safari to wrap the pixels around the image when they hit an edge. When this button is checked, any pixel which hits the edge of the image will be brought around the opposite side; thus, if a pixel is shifted off the top of the image, it will be brought around to the bottom and put back on. If the Wrap image? box is *not* checked, then any pixel which reaches the edge falls off and is lost.

Tools: Skew Tool

Selecting the Skew Tool menu entry brings up the Skew Tool dialog box, which allows you to set the features of the skew tool. Skewing an image is a process that allows you to *bend* the image (or currently selected portion) in a given direction by a certain amount. (See Figure 8–20.)

THE SKEW IMAGE DIALOG BOX How drastically the image is bent is controlled by the *skew angle,* which you set with the two angle edit controls and the vertical and horizontal scrollers. The higher the angle (up to a maximum of ±90 degrees), the greater the amount of skew that is applied.

Once you've chosen a skew angle, you can skew the image using the four skew buttons. For example, to skew the image left by 45 degrees, you would:

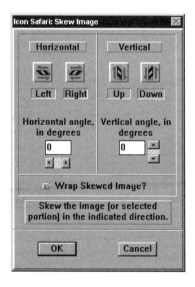

Figure 8–20 The Skew Tool Settings Dialog Box.

1. Enter 45 into the horizontal angle edit control, either by typing in the value 45, or using the scroller arrows.

2. Press the Left Skew button.

Pressing the Right Skew button would skew the image to the right by 45 degrees (in our example, pressing the Right Skew button would undo the effects of the Left Skew button).

THE OPTIONS MENU

The Options menu allows you to customize various aspects of the Icon Safari Editor to your own tastes. (See Figure 8–21.) The following menu entries are available:

Novice User	Sets user level to novice
Expert User	Sets user level to experienced
Reset to Default	Resets user selectable options to original settings
Show Mouse Position	Shows/hides mouse position display
Image Size	Sets the size of the image
Image Type	Sets the image type.

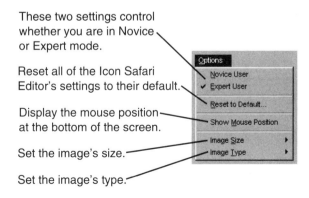

Figure 8–21 The Options Menu of the Icon Safari Editor.

Options: Novice User

Selecting the Novice User menu entry turns on a flag which causes the Icon Safari Editor to display various cautionary messages when you are about to perform an action which might be destructive or unexpected. For example, in Novice mode, when you click on the Full Clear tool button, the Editor will post a cautionary advisory first, asking you if you really want to clear the workspace.

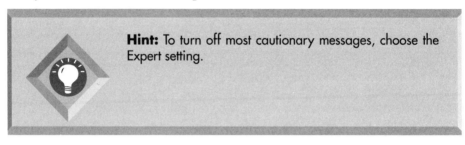

Hint: To turn off most cautionary messages, choose the Expert setting.

Options: Expert User

The Expert User setting allows you to turn off most of the Icon Safari Editor's warning messages; most actions, destructive or not, will simply be executed. (A few, such as file overwrites, will still generate a caution box.)

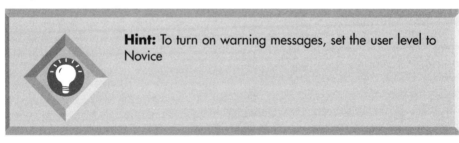

Hint: To turn on warning messages, set the user level to Novice

Options: Reset To Default...

This menu entry will reset all of the user selectable options in the Editor to their original default settings. This action occurs immediately.

Hint: You can experiment with what the different settings of the Editor do and then cancel your changes by using the Reset to Default menu command.

Options: Show Mouse Position

This menu entry toggles whether or not the mouse coordinates are displayed in the information line at the bottom of the screen. When a checkmark is displayed beside this menu entry, the mouse coordinates are shown; when no checkmark appears, then the mouse coordinates are not shown.

The mouse coordinates are defined as the pixel that the mouse is currently over when the mouse is in the Editing Grid. For example, the upper-left corner of the grid is pixel (1, 1). The bottom-left corner pixel is (32, 1), and so on.

Options: Image Size

This menu entry allows you to specify the size of the image in terms of pixels in both the horizontal (width) and vertical (height) directions. (See Figure 8–22.) There are several possibilities:

16x16	Creates an image that is 16 pixels high by 16 pixels wide
32x32	Creates an image that is 32 pixels high by 32 pixels wide
Custom Size	Displays a dialog box that allows you to define an image with custom values for its height and width.

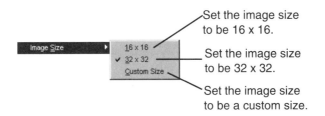

Set the image size
to be 16 x 16.

Set the image size
to be 32 x 32.

Set the image size
to be a custom size.

Figure 8–22 The Image Size Submenu of the Options Menu.

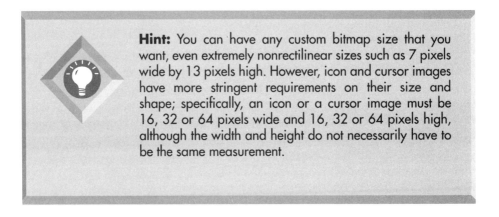

Hint: You can have any custom bitmap size that you want, even extremely nonrectilinear sizes such as 7 pixels wide by 13 pixels high. However, icon and cursor images have more stringent requirements on their size and shape; specifically, an icon or a cursor image must be 16, 32 or 64 pixels wide and 16, 32 or 64 pixels high, although the width and height do not necessarily have to be the same measurement.

Options: Image Type

This menu entry has a submenu associated with it that allows you to specify the nature of the image that you're editing. (See Figure 8–23.) Each image type has particular properties which are unique to it; cursors are monochrome but have an integral background mask which is displayed in two different colors. Icons can contain more than one image; bitmaps are not constrained to a particular size.

In general, you can switch images at any point, under certain conditions; however, the Editor may not let you change image types. If this happens, the Editor will usually give you a message informing you of the reason why you can't switch.

For example, you can't switch from a 16-color bitmap to a cursor image, because a cursor is not a color image. In this case, you must convert the colored pixels to either white or black before you can switch.

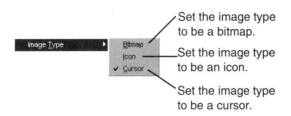

Figure 8–23 The Image Type Submenu of the Options Menu.

The Icon Menu

The Icon Menu contains commands which deal specifically with the manipulation of icon images. When you are editing an icon image (or images), this menu will be black, allowing you to select commands from it. For other types of images (cursors and bitmaps), this menu is grayed, and the commands are unavailable. (See Figure 8–24.)

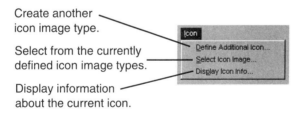

Figure 8–24 The Icon Menu of the Editor.

When you are editing an icon image, you have the following menu entries available to you:

Define Additional Icon...	Adds a new icon image to the current set
Select Icon Image...	Selects which icon image to edit
Display Icon Info...	Shows information about the current icon

Icon: Define Additional Icon

This menu entry allows you to add a new icon image to the current set of icon images. For more information about the different types of icon images, see Appendix B.

Clicking on this menu entry brings up a dialog box containing several controls which allow you to specify the height, width and number of colors for the new icon image. A list box is also displayed which shows you the currently defined icons. The icon which is shown in inverse video in the list box is the icon that you are currently editing. (See Figure 8–25.)

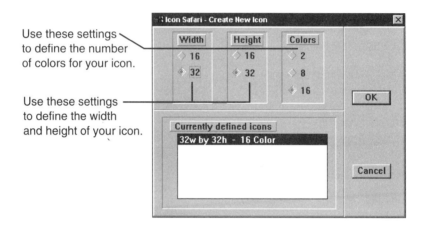

Use these settings to define the number of colors for your icon.

Use these settings to define the width and height of your icon.

Figure 8–25 The dialog box that lets you define additional icon images. You can define only one image of each type for a given icon.

To define a new icon choose its height, width and number of colors using the radio buttons and then click on OK.

Icon: Select Icon Image

This menu entry lets you choose which icon image you want to edit. For icons which have more than one image contained in them, this list box will display the properties of each icon; width in pixels, height in pixels and number of colors. To select an icon, either double-click on the desired entry, or single-click on the entry and then click on OK. (See Figure 8–26.)

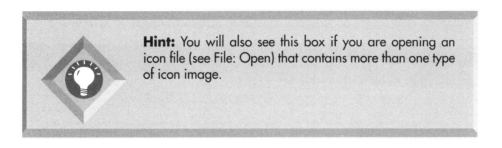

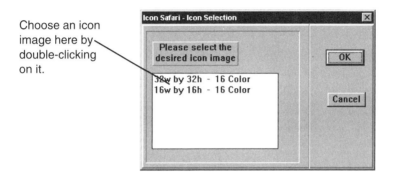

Choose an icon
image here by
double-clicking
on it.

Figure 8–26 The Icon Selection Dialog Box. You can choose between the
different icon images in your icon using this dialog.

Icon: Display Icon Info

This menu entry will bring up an information box that gives you the
width, height and number of colors of the icon image that you are currently editing. (See Figure 8–27.)

Figure 8–27 The Icon Information Dialog Box.

THE CURSOR MENU

The Cursor menu contains entries which deal specifically with editing cursors. When you are editing other image types (bitmaps and icons), this menu is grayed. See Figure 8–28 for a picture of the Cursor menu.

View HotSpot...	Views the current position of the hotspot
Set HotSpot...	Sets a new hotspot position
Test Cursor...	Tests how the cursor will look

View the current hotspot of the current cursor.

Set the hotspot of the current cursor.

Test how the cursor will look in action.

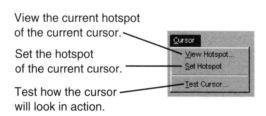

Figure 8–28 The Cursor Menu of the Editor.

Cursor: View Hotspot

The View HotSpot menu lets you see the current hotspot position of the cursor image and optionally set a new hotspot position, using a numerical entry dialog box. The hotspot is displayed as a medium gray pixel on the Editing Grid. (See Figure 8–29.)

To view the current hotspot, press View. If the hotspot is not visible, it may be because the dialog box is obscuring it. If this happens, you can move the dialog box to another portion of the screen.

CHANGING THE HOTSPOT Enter the new coordinates of the hotspot and then press View.

To keep the new hotspot, press OK; to cancel your changes, press Cancel.

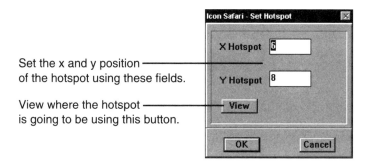

Set the x and y position
of the hotspot using these fields.

View where the hotspot
is going to be using this button.

Figure 8–29 The View Hotspot Dialog Box. You can set the hotspot and view it
from here.

Cursor: Set Hotspot

The Set Hotspot menu entry allows you to pick a new hotspot by clicking on the point at which you want the hotspot. Note that the hotspot is
set at the center of the hotspot cursor inside the circle.

 **The hotspot cursor.**

Cursor: Test Cursor

The Test Cursor menu lets you test how your cursor would appear in
action; this lets you create a cursor, and then test it out in a real dialog
box. (See Figure 8–30.)

As long as you move the cursor within the dialog box, you can see
how the cursor will appear in action. To close the dialog, click on OK.

THE HELP MENU

The Help menu contains two entries, Index and About Icon Safari (see
Figure 8–31).

Index will give you the index of the help system so you can look up
information about the Editor.

About Icon Safari will give you information about this product.

What your
cursor will look
like here.

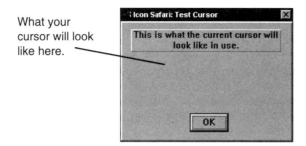

Figure 8–30 The Cursor Test Dialog Box. You can test out the appearance of your cursor here.

Figure 8–31 The Help Menu of the Editor.

What To Do
If Something
Goes Wrong

This section will help you if something goes wrong with the program, with your system, or if you just can't get something to work right.

PROBLEM The startup program doesn't run when I insert it into my CD-ROM drive.

1. Make sure the CD is clean and properly placed in the CD-ROM drive. If you can read the disk manually, but not automatically, this is not the problem.

2. Your CD-ROM driver may not be optimized for use with Windows 95. If this is the case, then the Autoplay feature of Windows 95 may not work. To verify if your CD-ROM is optimized for Windows 95, perform the following steps:
   a. Open the Windows 95 Control Panel folder and double-click on the System icon.
   b. Click on the Performance tab.

   If any of your hardware drivers are not fully optimized for use with Windows 95, they will be listed here with an explanation of the exact problem and suggestions on how to fix it. Optimization problems are usually caused by having real-mode DOS drivers loaded in your Config.sys or Autoexec.bat files. For further help, use the Troubleshooting Wizard.

3. Your CD-ROM Drive may not have detected that you put the Icon Safari CD in the drive. Select the Refresh option located in the View pull-down menu of your main hard drive window. When the Icon Safari icon appears, double-click on it. The setup program should appear.

4. The AutoPlay feature may be disabled. To check this, perform the following steps:
   a. Open the Windows 95 Control Panel folder and double-click on the System icon.
   b. Click on the Device Manager tab.
   c. Click on the plus sign located next to the CD-ROM icon.
   d. Highlight your CD-ROM drive and click on the Properties button.
   e. Click on the Settings tab.

   The Auto Insert Notification box should be checked. If it is not, then click on the checkbox to enable the AutoPlay feature.

PROBLEM I get intermittent system crashes when using Icon Safari. When I select Details I get a message similar to the following:

<Application> caused a general protection fault in module POPUP.DLL.

1. Some systems are not compatible with the pop-up program launcher in Icon Safari. If this is the case, you can disable the program launcher without affecting any of the other features of Icon Safari. Here's how to disable the pop-up program launcher:

   a. Start the Icon Safari Navigator.
   b. Select the system menu in the upper-left corner of the window.
   c. Select the Special Options menu entry. (See Figure 1–2 for a picture of this.)
   d. The Special Options dialog will appear. (See Figure 1–3 for a picture of this dialog.)
   e. Click on the Application Launcher enabled checkbox so that *no check mark appears.*
   f. Click on OK.
   g. A message will appear, telling you that any changes you've made won't take effect until the next time you start Icon Safari.
   h. Shut down the Icon Safari Navigator and then restart it.
   i. The pop-up program launcher will no longer appear. You should not experience any problems with unexplained system crashes after this. (At least, you won't experience any that are related to Icon Safari!)

PROBLEM When I apply a busy cursor in the Cursor Control Panel, it never seems to appear when I'm actually using the system. *Or* when I apply a busy cursor, it isn't drawn properly.

1. This indicates that your video driver may not be written properly or has a bug in it. You can change how Icon Safari draws the busy cursor from the Special Options panel.

   a. Start the Icon Safari Navigator.
   b. Select the system menu in the upper-left corner of the window.
   c. Select the Special Options menu entry. (See Figure 1–2 for a picture of this.)

  d. The Special Options dialog will appear. (See Figure 1–3 for a picture of this dialog.)
  e. Click on the check box Erase before redraw? so that a check mark appears in it.
  f. Click on OK.
  g. A message will appear, telling you that any changes you've made won't take effect until the next time you start Icon Safari.
  h. Shut down the Icon Safari Navigator and then restart it.

The busy cursor should now be working properly. If it does not, contact your video card manufacturer for an updated video driver or try switching to a generic video driver that comes with Windows95.

PROBLEM When I apply a busy cursor in the Cursor Control Panel, it causes the system to crash when the busy cursor is displayed.

  1. This indicates that your video driver has a bug in it. You can disable the use of the busy cursor in Icon Safari from the Special Options Panel.

  a. Start the Icon Safari Navigator.
  b. Select the system menu in the upper-left corner of the window.
  c. Select the Special Options menu entry. (See Figure 1–2 for a picture of this.)
  d. The Special Options dialog will appear. (See Figure 1–3 for a picture of this dialog.)
  e. Click on the check box Disable busy cursors? so that a check mark appears in it.
  f. Click on OK.
  g. A message will appear, telling you that any changes you've made won't take effect until the next time you start Icon Safari.
  h. Shut down the Icon Safari Navigator and then restart it.

The busy cursor is now disabled. You should not experience further problems with the busy cursor. If you change your video card, or update your driver, you may want to try turning this off to see if the driver has been fixed.

PROBLEM When I apply a busy cursor in the Cursor Control Panel, it displays very slowly. How can I speed it up?

1. You can change the speed of the busy cursor in Icon Safari from the Special Options Panel.

   a. Start the Icon Safari Navigator.
   b. Select the system menu in the upper-left corner of the window.
   c. Select the Special Options menu entry. (See Figure 1–2 for a picture of this.)
   d. The Special Options dialog will appear. (See Figure 1–3 for a picture of this dialog.)
   e. You can set the speed of the animation for the busy cursor by setting the number in the Timer speed (in mSeconds) box. You can click on the up and down arrows, which will increase or decrease the time, or you can type a number into the box directly. The number represents the number of milliseconds (1000ths of a second) before the next animation is played. In the default case, 900 mSeconds, or 9/10ths of a second elapse between each animation frame. You can speed this up by making this number smaller. You should not make this number smaller than 250, as it will adversely affect your system's performance.
   f. Click on OK.
   g. A message will appear, telling you that any changes you've made won't take effect until the next time you start Icon Safari.
   h. Shut down the Icon Safari Navigator and then restart it.

   The busy cursor will now animate at the new speed that you've chosen.

PROBLEM I have a sound assigned to the OK button, yet sometimes when I click on an OK button the sound is not played.

1. Icon Safari relies on an internal text field of buttons in order to be able to tell that a particular button has been pressed. In some buttons, this field does not contain the same text as the text which is actually displayed to you—thus, a button which appears to have the word OK in it might actually have something like ID_OK_BUTTON. In this case, Icon Safari cannot tell that the button is an OK button, and so will not play the correct sound.

B

About Icons

Icons are images which are displayed by the Windows desktop (or other desktops which are compatible with Windows Icons). An icon consists of two pieces: the foreground mask and the background mask.

The *foreground mask* is also referred to as the foreground image, or icon image. This is the color portion of the icon that the end user sees when Windows displays the icon.

What the end user does not see is the process by which the icon gets put onto the desktop. First, an image called the *background mask* is used to create a space where Windows can place the foreground image. It is the background mask which is responsible for clearing a space on the desktop where the foreground image will subsequently be placed. When Windows gets ready to display an icon on the screen, it first takes the background mask and uses it as a cookie cutter onto the desktop. For each pixel in the background mask which is black, Windows will clear a pixel on the desktop. If the pixel in the background mask is white, Windows does not change the desktop image.

Next, Windows takes the foreground image and lays it down into the space just created by the background mask. This is the final image that the user sees.

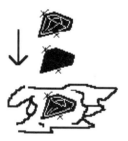

Foreground image (color)

Background image (monochrome)

Resulting desktop image

The Icon Safari Editor will automatically create a background mask for you as you edit the image. However, you may still want manual control of certain parts of the mask; this is what the transparent and inverse colors are used for.

When you want to create an area of the icon that is transparent (i.e., the background will show through), then you should use the transparent color to draw on the Editing Grid.

When you want to create an area of the icon that is inverse (i.e., the inverse color of the background will show through), then you should use the inverse color to draw on the Editing Grid.

Other than that, you don't have to do anything—the Editor takes care of all the ugly behind-the-scenes work necessary to make the proper image.

In addition to the foreground and background masks, an icon (as stored in an .ico file) can contain more than *one type* of icon image; it's possible for an icon to have a 32x32 by 16 color version, a 32x16 by 2 color version, and other resolutions and colors. The Icon Safari Editor, unlike some other icon editors, allows you to edit *all* the different versions of an icon from your current resolution (limited only by the number of colors that your system can display). This means that you can create a good looking icon regardless of the final destination of that icon. (To edit in color, you must, of course, have a color system.)

The Icon Safari Editor also does *not* create other resolution icons based on your current resolution; that is, if you create a VGA compatible icon (32 x 32 by 16 colors) and save it to a file, the Editor will *not* create a CGA compatible icon (32 x 16 by 2 colors) as well. The Editor saves only those icons which you have explicitly created. This means that if you expect an icon to run on systems with a resolution other than yours, you must hand create those icons yourself. It has been our experience that algorithms that purport to create other resolution icons usually do a poor job of it.

Index

• •

• •

LICENSE AGREEMENT AND LIMITED WARRANTY

READ THE FOLLOWING TERMS AND CONDITIONS CAREFULLY BEFORE OPENING THIS DISK PACKAGE. THIS LEGAL DOCUMENT IS AN AGREEMENT BETWEEN YOU AND PRENTICE-HALL, INC. (THE "COMPANY"). BY OPENING THIS SEALED DISK PACKAGE, YOU ARE AGREEING TO BE BOUND BY THESE TERMS AND CONDITIONS. IF YOU DO NOT AGREE WITH THESE TERMS AND CONDITIONS, DO NOT OPEN THE DISK PACKAGE. PROMPTLY RETURN THE UNOPENED DISK PACKAGE AND ALL ACCOMPANYING ITEMS TO THE PLACE YOU OBTAINED THEM FOR A FULL REFUND OF ANY SUMS YOU HAVE PAID.

1.   **GRANT OF LICENSE:** In consideration of your payment of the license fee, which is part of the price you paid for this product, and your agreement to abide by the terms and conditions of this Agreement, the Company grants to you a nonexclusive right to use and display the copy of the enclosed software program (hereinafter the "SOFTWARE") on a single computer (i.e., with a single CPU) at a single location so long as you comply with the terms of this Agreement. The Company reserves all rights not expressly granted to you under this Agreement.

2.   **OWNERSHIP OF SOFTWARE:** You own only the magnetic or physical media (the enclosed disks) on which the SOFTWARE is recorded or fixed, but the Company retains all the rights, title, and ownership to the SOFTWARE recorded on the original disk copy(ies) and all subsequent copies of the SOFTWARE, regardless of the form or media on which the original or other copies may exist. This license is not a sale of the original SOFTWARE or any copy to you.

3.   **COPY RESTRICTIONS:** This SOFTWARE and the accompanying printed materials and user manual (the "Documentation") are the subject of copyright. You may not copy the Documentation or the SOFTWARE, except that you may make a single copy of the SOFT-WARE for backup or archival purposes only. You may be held legally responsible for any copying or copyright infringement which is caused or encouraged by your failure to abide by the terms of this restriction.

4.   **USE RESTRICTIONS:** You may not network the SOFTWARE or otherwise use it on more than one computer or computer terminal at the same time. You may physically transfer the SOFTWARE from one computer to another provided that the SOFTWARE is used on only one computer at a time. You may not distribute copies of the SOFTWARE or Documentation to others. You may not reverse engineer, disassemble, decompile, modify, adapt, translate, or create derivative works based on the SOFTWARE or the Documentation without the prior written consent of the Company.

5.   **TRANSFER RESTRICTIONS:** The enclosed SOFTWARE is licensed only to you and may not be transferred to any one else without the prior written consent of the Company. Any unauthorized transfer of the SOFTWARE shall result in the immediate termination of this Agreement.

6.   **TERMINATION:** This license is effective until terminated. This license will terminate automatically without notice from the Company and become null and void if you fail to comply with any provisions or limitations of this license. Upon termination, you shall destroy the Documentation and all copies of the SOFTWARE. All provisions of this Agreement as to warranties, limitation of liability, remedies or damages, and our ownership rights shall survive termination.

7.   **MISCELLANEOUS:** This Agreement shall be construed in accordance with the laws of the United States of America and the State of New York and shall benefit the Company, its affiliates, and assignees.

8.   **LIMITED WARRANTY AND DISCLAIMER OF WARRANTY:** The Company warrants that the SOFTWARE, when properly used in accordance with the Documentation, will operate in substantial conformity with the description of the SOFTWARE set forth in the Documentation. The Company does not warrant that the SOFTWARE will meet your requirements or that the operation of the SOFTWARE will be uninterrupted or error-free. The Company warrants that the media on which the SOFTWARE is delivered shall be free from defects in materials and workmanship under normal use for a period of thirty (30) days from the date of your purchase. Your only remedy and the Company's only obligation under these limited

warranties is, at the Company's option, return of the warranted item for a refund of any amounts paid by you or replacement of the item. Any replacement of SOFTWARE or media under the warranties shall not extend the original warranty period. The limited warranty set forth above shall not apply to any SOFTWARE which the Company determines in good faith has been subject to misuse, neglect, improper installation, repair, alteration, or damage by you. EXCEPT FOR THE EXPRESSED WARRANTIES SET FORTH ABOVE, THE COMPANY DISCLAIMS ALL WARRANTIES, EXPRESS OR IMPLIED, INCLUDING WITHOUT LIMITATION, THE IMPLIED WARRANTIES OF MERCHANTABILITY AND FITNESS FOR A PARTICULAR PURPOSE. EXCEPT FOR THE EXPRESS WARRANTY SET FORTH ABOVE, THE COMPANY DOES NOT WARRANT, GUARANTEE, OR MAKE ANY REPRESENTATION REGARDING THE USE OR THE RESULTS OF THE USE OF THE SOFTWARE IN TERMS OF ITS CORRECTNESS, ACCURACY, RELIABILITY, CURRENTNESS, OR OTHERWISE.

IN NO EVENT, SHALL THE COMPANY OR ITS EMPLOYEES, AGENTS, SUPPLI-ERS, OR CONTRACTORS BE LIABLE FOR ANY INCIDENTAL, INDIRECT, SPECIAL, OR CONSEQUENTIAL DAMAGES ARISING OUT OF OR IN CONNECTION WITH THE LICENSE GRANTED UNDER THIS AGREEMENT, OR FOR LOSS OF USE, LOSS OF DATA, LOSS OF INCOME OR PROFIT, OR OTHER LOSSES, SUSTAINED AS A RESULT OF INJURY TO ANY PERSON, OR LOSS OF OR DAMAGE TO PROPERTY, OR CLAIMS OF THIRD PARTIES, EVEN IF THE COMPANY OR AN AUTHORIZED REPRE-SENTATIVE OF THE COMPANY HAS BEEN ADVISED OF THE POSSIBILITY OF SUCH DAMAGES. IN NO EVENT SHALL LIABILITY OF THE COMPANY FOR DAM-AGES WITH RESPECT TO THE SOFTWARE EXCEED THE AMOUNTS ACTUALLY PAID BY YOU, IF ANY, FOR THE SOFTWARE.

SOME JURISDICTIONS DO NOT ALLOW THE LIMITATION OF IMPLIED WAR-RANTIES OR LIABILITY FOR INCIDENTAL, INDIRECT, SPECIAL, OR CONSEQUEN-TIAL DAMAGES, SO THE ABOVE LIMITATIONS MAY NOT ALWAYS APPLY. THE WARRANTIES IN THIS AGREEMENT GIVE YOU SPECIFIC LEGAL RIGHTS AND YOU MAY ALSO HAVE OTHER RIGHTS WHICH VARY IN ACCORDANCE WITH LOCAL LAW.

ACKNOWLEDGMENT

YOU ACKNOWLEDGE THAT YOU HAVE READ THIS AGREEMENT, UNDER-STAND IT, AND AGREE TO BE BOUND BY ITS TERMS AND CONDITIONS. YOU ALSO AGREE THAT THIS AGREEMENT IS THE COMPLETE AND EXCLUSIVE STATEMENT OF THE AGREEMENT BETWEEN YOU AND THE COMPANY AND SUPERSEDES ALL PROPOSALS OR PRIOR AGREEMENTS, ORAL, OR WRITTEN, AND ANY OTHER COMMUNICATIONS BETWEEN YOU AND THE COMPANY OR ANY REPRESENTATIVE OF THE COMPANY RELATING TO THE SUBJECT MATTER OF THIS AGREEMENT.

Should you have any questions concerning this Agreement or if you wish to contact the Company for any reason, please contact in writing at the address below or call the at the tele-phone number provided.

PTR Customer Service
Prentice Hall PTR
One Lake Street
Upper Saddle River, New Jersey 07458
Telephone: 201-236-7105